WE GREW UP TOGETHER

Broken Glass Book Series - Volume #1: The Red Book

WE GREW UP TOGETHER

A Teen Parent's Journey to Healing,

Restoration and the discovery

of God's unfailing LOVE

Thelma R. Davis-Clanton

We Grew Up Together
Broken Glass Book Series - Volume #1: The Red Book

Copyright © 2025 by Thelma R. Davis-Clanton
Published by **Fragments of Faith Publishing**

All rights reserved. No part of this publication may be reproduced, distributed, or transmitted in any form or by any means, including photocopying, recording, or other electronic or mechanical methods, without the prior written permission of the author, except in the case of brief quotations embodied in reviews and certain other noncommercial uses permitted by copyright law.

Scripture quotations are taken from the Holy Bible, New International Version® (NIV®).
Copyright © 1973, 1978, 1984, 2011 by Biblica, Inc.™
Used by permission. All rights reserved worldwide.

This is a work of nonfiction. The events, experiences, and reflections described are based on the author's life. Some names and identifying details may have been adjusted to protect the privacy of individuals.

For permission requests, contact the author at: docdavisclanton25@gmail.com
ISBN: 979-8-9942947-0-3
ISBN: 979-8-9942947-2-7

Cover Design: **Fragments of Faith Publishing**
Printed in the United States of America

The Broken Glass Book Series

Series Introduction

Have you ever been cut by a piece of glass?
Better yet, imagine this: you're at home, moving quickly, when suddenly a glass plate slips from your hands and crashes onto the hardwood floor.

It shatters, tiny shards scattering in every direction. What's the first thing you do? You warn everyone nearby to stay back so they don't step on the glass.

The next step is to gather the larger pieces carefully, placing them into a thick bag so they won't cut through.
Finally, you reach for the broom and dustpan to sweep up the smaller fragments.

I mention these steps intentionally because there's meaning behind them. Why don't we simply collect all the broken pieces, lay them on the table, and try to glue the plate back together? Because it's not that simple. It's far more complicated than it looks. And even after you've cleaned everything up, somehow months or even years later, you'll still find a tiny shard of glass tucked away in a corner, a quiet reminder of what was once broken.

When I think about broken glass, I think about the parts of us that can't be easily repaired. I think about my own brokenness, how complex, painful, and scattered it has been, and how only God has the power to make me whole again. That's why I named this series *"Broken Glass."*

Broken glass doesn't just represent brokenness; it represents pain, danger, and persistence. The shards of glass scatter everywhere. They're sharp. Some are so small you can't even see them, but those are the ones that cut the deepest.

In this journey called life, I've tried to gather my shattered pieces and mend myself, only to realize that my own efforts were never enough. Each attempt left me facing the same truth: only God can truly restore what's broken. What was once broken can be whole again, only through the love and protection of our Lord and Savior.

So, I invite you to walk with me on this journey of discovery in an attempt to heal together. Bear witness as I sift through the fragments of my life, seeking to become whole and for my story to heal and save someone else.

"My sacrifice, O God, is a broken spirit; a broken and contrite heart you, God, will not despise."- Psalm 51:17

About This Volume

Volume One: The <u>Red</u> Book – We Grew Up Together

In *Broke Glass: The Red Book*, the first memoir in a powerful series, the author takes readers on an emotional journey through the shards of her tumultuous childhood and the complexities of navigating teen parenting. With raw honesty and vivid storytelling, she reflects on a childhood marked by challenges and uncertainty, revealing the perseverance and strength that shaped her journey. As she confronts the emotional scars of her past, the memoir also explores the unexpected discovery of God's presence amid heartache. Through guided prayers and intimate reflections, the author shares not only the obstacles she faced but also the resilience and courage she found within herself. *Broke Glass: The Red Book* is a moving testament to the power of healing and the courage it takes to reclaim one's story from the broken pieces of the past.

<u>The Color Red Represents:</u> Survival, Danger, Intensity, Power, Strength, Endurance, Love, Sacrifice, Courage.

Dedication

I dedicate my life to the Lord, giving all glory and honor to God. Thank you for seeing fit to bless me to wear many hats, including that of mother and wife. Your grace has carried me through seasons I didn't think I'd survive.

To my loving husband, Coley, thank you for being my constant. Your strength, support, and unwavering belief in me have helped me stand firm in who I am and who I am becoming. You are my rock. To my beautiful children, Ty-Queal, Lamar, Anastasia, Angelis, and Coley Jr., you are each a piece of my heart, and being your mother is one of my greatest joys. And to my grandson, Koa, your light reminds me every day of God's promises across generations. Being your Mom-Mom is a blessing beyond words.

This book, this journey, this healing, it's a direct reflection of the love y'all have shown me.

With a grateful heart,
Thelma

Personal Reflection

I am....

As I reflect on this first book in my *Broken Glass* series, I find myself looking beyond the woman I am today and into the little girl still living inside me. A few phrases come to mind that begin to describe me, both then and now. Some reflect who I once was; others speak to who I've grown to be.

I am talkative, yet sometimes shy. I am loving and tend to love hard, though I've learned not everyone welcomes that level of love. I'm a protector at heart. I am a thinker, sometimes overthinking. I am a giver and provider, sometimes to a fault. I am imperfect and deeply flawed. I am strong-minded, yet I have weak moments too. And most of all, I am a child of the King, which makes me royalty. This reflection gives just a snippet of all the layers that make me who I am. I have come to the realization that I am broken, and I will never *not* need God.

"The Lord is close to the brokenhearted and saves those who are crushed in spirit." - Psalm 34:18

Content Warning

This memoir shares my lived experiences of growing up in poverty, early sexual exposure, and teen motherhood. These stories are told as part of my journey toward understanding, healing, and resilience. Some content may be triggering or difficult for readers who have experienced similar circumstances. Please read with care and extend yourself grace along the way. I encourage you to honor your emotional needs as you read, taking pauses and returning when you feel ready.

Contents

Preface: ....*xi*

Introduction: *A Slice of the Pie* *1*

Chapter 1: *Honey on My Ears* *7*

Chapter 2: *Deep Tangled Roots* *12*

Chapter 3: *A Teen Mother's Love, Passed Down* *17*

Chapter 4: *From Stepdad to Dad: Love Passed Down* *23*

Chapter 5: *A Teen Father's Love, Passed Down* *30*

Chapter 6: *Innocence Interrupted* *39*

Chapter 7: *Guilt and Shame of Teen Sex* *45*

Chapter 8: *Unwrapping My New Reality* *53*

Chapter 9: *He's Here: Now What?* 58

Chapter 10: *Looking for Love in All the Wrong Places* ...66

Chapter 11: *A Vow to My Three Stoogents* 75

Chapter 12: *The Growing Pains of Leadership* 81

Chapter 13: *My Full Circle Moment* 88

Chapter 14: *Motherhood Lessons* 97

Chapter 15: *Generational Trauma Responses* 104

Chapter 16: *Memory Lane* 110

Chapter 17: *Purpose, Faith, & Your Journey Forward*..117

Author's Note: 125

Preface

My Inspiration to Write This Memoir

If someone had handed me a book like this when I was 14, I would've clung to it like my life depended on it, because in many ways, it did.

I wrote *We Grew Up Together* for every teenage girl who's ever stared at a positive pregnancy test with trembling hands and a thousand thoughts racing through her mind. I wrote it for the young boys who are trying to figure out what it means to become a father while still figuring out who they are themselves. I wrote it for the teen who's feeling ashamed, the one hiding their truth, and the one who doesn't know how to ask for help. I wrote it for the adult parents who initially didn't know how to parent because no one ever taught them. And I wrote it for the little girl inside of me who never stopped searching for love, safety, and answers.

This is not a perfect story. It's not wrapped in a bow or tied up with neat lessons. But it's real. It's full of pain, beauty, growth, and most of all, hope.

Through the Broken Glass series, my goal in sharing my testimony is to help others see that even shattered pieces can reflect light. Even broken things can be made whole again.

If you are or ever were a teen parent, a product of generational trauma, or simply someone trying to make sense of where you came from and where you're going, you belong here.

I see you.

I was you.

And know that there is still purpose in your story.

"In between suffocation and surrender,
don't give up in the middle." – Thelma Davis-Clanton

Introduction

Slice of the Pie

Before you step into the earliest chapters of my life, I want to offer you a small window into the woman who sits behind these words. A slice of the pie:

Still becoming: I am many things: wife, mother, creator, believer, survivor, but I didn't become any of these overnight. My story is layered, stretched across years of lessons, losses, and unexpected blessings, which is why I chose to break my memoir into a series. However, what you'll read in this particular memoir is only the beginning, the first part of a longer journey that shaped the woman I am still becoming.

Space to breathe: I grew up in Philadelphia, PA. Home wasn't always consistent. Safety wasn't guaranteed. Some days felt calm enough to catch my breath, and other days felt like walking on thin ice, never knowing when the surface underneath me would crack. That inconsistency taught me early how to observe, how to survive, and how to take the world seriously very early on. But, still, even in the middle of everything I lacked, God found ways to give me space to breathe.

I found refuge outside: During my middle school years, I remember joining the Blue Lightning Drill Team. This opportunity was the much-needed escape from my life's reality. When we marched through the neighborhood with the drummers, our rhythms echoed off the rowhomes and pulled people out onto their porches. For those few hours, I wasn't worried about home. I wasn't worried about expectations. I was just a little girl moving in sync with something larger than herself. My dedication made me co-captain, then captain. Our leader, a Christian woman with a calm presence, would find creative ways to teach us scripture while she taught us dance formation. At the time, I didn't realize how deeply her words were planting themselves in me. Looking back now, I realize refuge was found, and I see her as one of the first women to water the seed of faith God placed in my heart.

Survival was my portion: Growing up with teenage parents came with realities. I'll share more deeply later in this book, but what I can say here is that their youth shaped my foundation. And in a pattern neither planned nor understood, I became a teenage mother myself. I didn't know it then, but God was already shaping my strength. As you will later learn throughout my book series, there were years of domestic violence and years of trying to hold myself together for the sake of my children, who depended on me. You, holding this book today, are a direct result of my survival. Because survival is my portion, and God is with me, I now have the freedom and the courage to tell my story.

"When you pass through the waters, I will be with you." - Isaiah 43:2

Childcare chose me: My career began during high school in the most unexpected way, dropping my son and daughter off at daycare and not wanting to leave them. Instead of walking out, I asked if they were hiring. That one question turned into over twenty years in childcare, years of nurturing other people's children with the same care I poured into my own. Every time a child learned something I taught them, every time I saw growth that came from my patience and presence, I felt a quiet confirmation from God. I was able to boldly step into purpose; I realize now that childcare chose me.

That long road to identity: During my years as a single mother, raising three children alone was both my burden and my blessing. They were my peace, my motivation, and the reason I kept going when I wanted to collapse. I learned that I was capable of loving beyond flaws, capable of rebuilding from nothing, and capable of surviving what was meant to break me. It wasn't an easy road, but a necessary road that shaped my identity.

The consistency I needed was Him: My return to Christ in my early twenties came after the storm. When the noise finally quieted, and the walls I had leaned on fell away, God became the steady presence I could trust. I began seeking Him in everything, from my smallest decisions to the moments that determined the direction of my life. And the more I leaned into Him, the more I realized He had been holding me long before I understood His voice. He held the consistency I needed all along.

It's just how I love: Today, I am a wife, almost ten years into building a blended family. Blending families is its own journey, a mixture of joy, challenges, and lessons in grace. Co-parenting hasn't always been easy, but with God's support, we continue growing, learning, and finding our rhythm. Outside of motherhood and work, I am a creative soul. My family calls me "extra," and I've learned to embrace it. I love colors, themes, décor, celebrations, and the art of bringing visions to life. My world is color-coordinated, not for perfection but for peace. It's how I stay organized, how I stay grounded, and how I keep order in a life that once felt unpredictable. I pour into others, encourage them to pursue their dreams, and show up with love and intentionality. Planning is not just what I do, it's how I love.

Are you ready to flip the pages? This introduction was just a piece of my story, a small slice before the deeper chapters begin. There are chapters, other books, and seasons yet to come, but I pray that this introduction gave you a glimpse of who I truly am. And my prayer is that as you read this book, you will feel the heartbeat behind every word. You will bear witness as I reclaim my life, one word at a time. I hope you see not just where I've been, but the God who carried me through it all. And that somewhere in my story, you find encouragement for yourself. Every memory, every lesson, and every scar carries a purpose far greater than the pain that shaped them. I hope you're ready to flip the page, because next is where the story truly begins.

Welcome to my journey......

"The journey of a thousand miles begins with a single step."-- Lao Tz

Chapter

1

Honey On My Ears

I am the firstborn of three children on my mother's side and two on my father's, born and raised in Philadelphia, PA. With that "oldest child" position came pressure, the pressure to lead, to carry the load, and to be the example. For as long as I can remember, my mother has had high expectations of me. I wasn't just expected to know better; I was expected to be better. Growing up, if one of my younger siblings got in trouble, it always circled back, and somehow, I was in trouble. "Nay Nay, you know better," she'd say. And so, at a young age, I became an overthinker instead of a doer, at least when someone was watching. I internalized the message that I had to be the responsible one, even when I didn't feel ready for that weight. Those early expectations shaped the way I viewed myself long before I could even spell my own name.

"Before I even knew my name, the world was already telling me who I had to be." - Unknown

If I could go back to my earliest memory as a child, it would be the moment a bee stung me in my ear. I remember being in the schoolyard at TM Pierce Elementary School. It was early morning, and I was standing in line with my classmates, waiting to go inside for the day. I was in the first grade. I remember wearing a brand-new pair of gold stud earrings and feeling excited to show them off. What I didn't realize was that a bee had landed right on my ear. By the time I heard the buzzing, it was too late; it had already stung me. I screamed and cried in shock!

Tears rolled down my face as the sting flared and the buzzing faded. I cried so hard. The pain, the shock, the confusion of it all. I was taken into the building and checked out by the school nurse. I don't remember much about the rest of that day, but I do remember how exposed I felt, how something so small could cause so much pain. Looking back, that moment says a lot about who I was, even then: sensitive, observant, and deeply affected by the unexpected. I didn't always know how to protect myself, and I often didn't see things coming until they were already

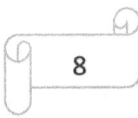

hurting me.

I think moments like this stay with us not just because of the pain, but because of what they reveal. Early on, we begin to learn that the world can hurt us in ways we don't see coming. That bee sting wasn't just about a sharp pain in my ear; it was a moment that mirrored a larger truth I didn't yet know how to describe. I was just a little girl standing in line, proud of my new gold studs, wanting to be noticed for something good. But instead, it was the opposite. I was noticed for being hurt.

A teacher knelt beside me, her voice calm but distant, "Hold still, sweetheart.
You're okay."

But I didn't feel okay. I felt exposed. And in a way, I was. Little did she know, my home life was filled with uncertainty, my parents struggling with substances, and my father was more gone than he was present. Looking back now, I can see that even in those early moments of pain and confusion, God had His hand on me. I didn't understand it then, but He was already teaching me something about His protection and presence, even in the middle of hurt.

"He heals the brokenhearted and binds up their wounds." -

Psalm 147:3

Experiences like that stay lodged in the body, especially for a child who's already living in quiet chaos. Throughout the years, I have learned that the brain remembers what it feels; it remembers pain, confusion, and abandonment, not always in full scenes, but in flashes and sensations.

I don't remember what we were learning that day or who I stood next to in line. But I remember how that one sting made me feel singled out, like I had been marked by something invisible. Just like at home, where things happened without warning, raised voices, disappearing parents, and empty promises. That bee became more than just a bug. It was a symbol of how unpredictable and unfair life could be. And even as the sting faded, the lesson didn't: sometimes, you don't see the hurt coming until it's already landed. Even while writing this chapter, the memories of that sting are still vivid. I can almost feel the burn of it, but I thank God for His healing power. I didn't know it then, but the same God who saw me that morning in the schoolyard would one day show me the depth of His love through grace and restoration.

Thelma R. Davis-Clanton

A Prayer for the Little Child Within

Father God,
I thank You for seeing the little child inside of me. The one who still remembers the pain, the confusion, and the moments I didn't understand. You were there even then, watching over me when I felt unseen.

Thank You for never leaving me, even when I didn't yet know how to look for You. In Isaiah 61:1, You said that "You have come to bind up the brokenhearted and to set the captives free".

Today, I bring you the parts of me that still feel bound by fear, shame, or memories I've carried far too long. Heal those tender places and bring freedom to my heart where pain once lived.

In Ezekiel 36:26, you also promised to give me a new heart and put a new spirit within me. Lord, I invite You to do just that! Renew my heart from the inside out. Teach me to love and comfort the child within me the way You always intended. Give me patience, grace, and compassion for others.

In Jesus' name I pray,
Amen

Chapter

2

Deep Tangled Roots

I didn't fully understand it at the time, but our family roots were already tangled with unhealthy generational patterns. Teenage pregnancies, substance struggles, and unspoken trauma were all quietly passed down, one branch at a time. I now see that these weren't isolated events. They were inherited behaviors, often rooted in pain that had never been fully healed.

My mother became pregnant with me while she was still in high school herself. She was just sixteen. My father was fifteen. They both carried the entanglements of their individual families. As teenagers, neither of them had the tools, the knowledge, or the emotional capacity to raise a child- not in the way a child deserves. But still, they tried, realizing that they, too, were still children trying to grow up. Later, that would shape the type of parenting I would receive.

"Families are like branches on a tree. We all grow in different directions, yet our roots remain as one." – Unknown

In my mother's early twenties, I recall the presence of family members stepping in, offering shelter or support when they could. On the flip side, I remember having an uncle and other family members living with us at times. The lack of stability wasn't something new for my family. I slowly started to understand that I am not the first in my bloodline to face homelessness and challenges early on. I come from a long line of survivors, some of whom didn't give up, even when the odds were stacked against them. As I got older, I began to notice more and understand more.

I witnessed several of my uncles, a few aunts, and older cousins struggling with addiction, whether to alcohol or drugs. Their behavior wasn't unusual in our world; it was part of the background noise of life. Parties, drinking, and loud music filled the homes, often lasting well into the night. What didn't always make it into the light of day were the arguments, the fights, and the emotional fallout that followed. After the drinking came the shouting, sometimes even physical altercations between family members. As children, we were often left to ourselves, unsupervised and unprotected, our curiosity left unchecked, our innocence exposed to things far beyond our years.

I remember being aware of sex before I truly understood what it was. Not because anyone talked to us about it, but because it was simply present, in conversations we overheard, in things we saw, in the silence where protection should have been. We weren't guided through childhood; we survived it.

That environment, one of instability, unaddressed pain, and blurred boundaries, shaped much of what I believed was normal. What is now widely seen as unhealthy or traumatic was, for us, just life. We didn't have the language to name what we were living through. We only had each other, cousins, siblings, and kids navigating chaos with no compass.

And as I reflect, now, I realize: the dysfunction didn't start with us. It was such an entanglement! It ran deeper, rooted in generations before us, generations that were traumatized, silenced, oppressed, and often doing the best they could with what little they had been given. The generations before us loved in ways they knew how, even if those ways were broken.

The more I learn, the more I understand that healing isn't just for me, it's for everyone who came before me and everyone who will come after. I carry their stories, their scars, and also the opportunity to do something different.

"You will know the truth, and the truth will set you free." - John 8:32

Coming to terms with your history can be painful, especially when that history includes things like undiagnosed mental health, domestic violence, teen pregnancy, absent fathers, abandonment, molestation, homelessness, or other cycles of emotional silence. But truth also opens the door to healing. And that's what this journey is about: telling the truth, honoring it, and choosing to grow anyway.

A Prayer for Healing Generational Patterns

Dear Heavenly Father,
Thank You for being a God of grace, mercy, and restoration. Thank you for seeing me, not just who I am today, but who I've been, and who I'm becoming. Lord, I bring before You the pain I inherited, the burdens I've carried, and the patterns I've seen repeat through the generations of my family of origin.

You know the things that have shaped me, the shame, the guilt, the silent struggles, the broken places, and the deep-rooted fears I've sometimes tried to hide.
But today, I choose to surrender it all to You.

Break every generational cycle that does not align with Your purpose for my life. Heal the places in me that were wounded before I even knew they were bleeding.

Father Gid, help me be the one who plants new seeds; seeds of peace, hope, wisdom, and healing, for the generations to come. Give me strength to walk in truth, courage to parent with love and grace, and faith to believe that change is not only possible, but already in motion. Lord, make me the chain-breaker in my family.

In Jesus' name I pray,
Amen

Chapter

3

A Mother's Love Passed Down

My mother is the middle child of three on her mother's side and the middle child of three on her father's side. As I grew older and became more curious about her upbringing, I began to ask questions, slowly piecing together the history that shaped her. I learned that as a young girl under her mother's care, she experienced both abuse and neglect. Eventually, her father stepped in and removed her and her brother from that environment, raising them with the help of his wife at the time. It was during those teenage years, while living with her father, that she met my biological father and later became pregnant with me.

I wouldn't say I had the best childhood. It wasn't perfect or carefree. But one thing I know for sure is that my journey has led me to be the powerhouse of a mother that I am today. I was protected and shown love in the only ways my parents knew how to express it.

From as early as I can remember, alcohol touched many of the homes we lived in. My mother drank beer often, a habit that seemed to carry the weight of her past, but even in that, her love for us was never in question.

"He lifted me out of the slimy pit, out of the mud and mire; he set my feet on a rock and gave me a firm place to stand. He put a new song in my mouth, a hymn of praise to our God." - Psalm 40:2-3

Even under the haze of alcohol, my mother found ways to comfort us. She was bubbly, full of life in moments of joy, perhaps covering the pain she carried from her own childhood. She would play music, smoke her cigarettes, and somehow make our house feel alive, warm, and safe.

Her encouragement wasn't loud or demanding, but quiet and steady, instilling in me a drive and determination to finish school, to succeed, to rise. I now see that her gentle guidance, combined with her perseverance, was a model of love for my siblings and me, even when she struggled with her own battles. My mother was just a teenager when she became a mother herself. I can imagine how she carried the weight of fear, uncertainty, and sacrifice. She gave up parts of her own childhood, comforts, and freedom to protect and nurture her children. Every move, every decision, was made to keep us together and safe. Though life was far from easy, I always knew that being with her meant being home, no matter where we physically lived. And even in those times, I now understand that God's presence never left us.

"Even when I walk through the darkest valley, I will not be afraid, for you are close beside me. Your rod and your staff protect and comfort me." - Psalm 23:4

My mother's upbringing shaped her in profound ways. She was a daddy's girl at heart, deeply bonded to my grandfather Allen, who raised her for much of her life. I vividly remember the time he came to stay with us during his recovery from stage 3 throat cancer. He had endured major surgery to remove the cancer, wearing a bar across his face to hold his jaw and eating only through a feeding tube. Despite his condition, he still tried to smoke cigarettes and even attempted to sneak corn liquor into his feeding tube, determined to drink. At the time, I can tell my mother was frustrated with him, hoping he would stop, but also compassionate, realizing he was older and set in his ways.

Watching my grandfather struggle and decline left a deep impression on her, and on me. She had seen the fragility of life and the grip of addiction firsthand, and it made her more determined to protect her own children from similar pain. When we received the call that he had passed away, it was a heavy grief, a loss that left her and all of us reeling. And yet, even in this sorrow, I saw the depth of her love and resilience. She learned to navigate heartbreak while still showing up for those she loved, a lesson in grace and perseverance that would guide me throughout my life.

"Sometimes love doesn't come wrapped in comfort. Sometimes it shows up in survival." – Unknown

Over the years, I also came to understand that, despite the pain she endured, my mother still carried love for her mother. In adulthood, after years of sobriety, she sought therapy, worked toward healing, and made the intentional choice to forgive. At the time, with only one living parent, she did her best to rebuild a relationship with my grandmother. She worked hard to rebuild that relationship, and thankfully, it lasted until my grandmother's passing. I never forget the day she transitioned; my mother was heartbroken, but I also recall her saying how grateful she was to have found peace, to have forgiven her mother, and to have spent precious time with her leading up to her final days.

As I reflect on my childhood, I understand why she was so determined to keep us safe and together. There were times we moved from place to place, staying with different family members. I remember sleeping on floors, couches, and pull-out beds, yet the presence of my mother always made those temporary spaces feel like home. Her commitment to us, despite her struggles, is a testament to her love and strength.

Looking back now, I realize just how deeply her strength ran. Though alcoholism wrapped itself around her, it never broke her bond with her children. She didn't run from motherhood, even when life was heavy. Even when losing her own parents. Her love, her sacrifices, her determination, all of it was passed down to me. And as a parent now myself, I pray that my children have felt this same level of love and protection.

A Prayer for those carrying Mother Wounds

Dear God,
You know the places in me that still ache from what I didn't receive. You know how deeply I wanted her to be there, for the hugs, the advice, the safety, the love.

Sometimes, I wonder what I did wrong. Sometimes, I grieve the mother I never truly had, or the one I lost too soon, whether physically or emotionally. And now, as a parent myself, I feel that gap even more.

Lord, help me to release the guilt that was never mine to carry. Heal the child in me who still looks for her. Remind me that her absence does not define my worth, and that I am not destined to repeat her mistakes. Give me the courage to mother my children differently, to show up, even when I feel like I'm still learning how. Where there was neglect, help me plant nurture. Where there was silence, let me speak love. Where there was pain, let Your healing overflow.

You are the God who sees me, who parents me with compassion, and who never abandons. Thank You for becoming what I didn't have, and for walking with me as I become everything my children need.
Amen

Chapter

4

From Stepdad to Dad: Love Passed Down

My stepfather is the youngest of two on his mother's side and the oldest of three from his father. He was initially raised in a single-parent home by his mother until she later married. During my mother's early teenage years, after becoming pregnant with my sister, she moved out of my grandfather's house and into a home shared with my stepfather and his mother. After moving out of my grandmother's house, I always remember my stepfather being in the picture, even when I didn't physically see him.

Growing up in the household, as a child, I didn't have words for what I was witnessing. I only knew that something shifted when my stepfather came in and out of the bathroom repeatedly. His appearance would change. His energy would change. He sounded different. I didn't understand why, and no one explained it to me at the time. I just knew that when he emerged, the man I knew felt distant and unfamiliar. Years later, I came to understand that he was under the influence of crack cocaine, but as a child, all I could sense was the change, the feeling that something had entered our home that I could not name.

Addiction was a constant presence in our home. He would leave from time to time, going in and out of rehabs, always returning with hope that things would change. During my early years, there was one period when he left and stayed gone longer than before. I noticed the shift immediately. My mother struggled deeply, and her addiction worsened. The house felt unstable, and everything seemed uncertain.

As I process and write this chapter, a very vivid memory comes to the surface. One evening, I was awakened out of my sleep and told that we had to leave the house and go to my grandmother's, his mother's, who at the time lived across the street. As I came down the stairs, the adults tried to move my siblings and me out quickly, while covering our eyes, but I looked anyway. I saw puddles of blood on the dining room table; it looked like thick puddles of spaghetti sauce, along with shattered shards of glass from a broken 40-ounce beer bottle. I froze, unsure of what had happened or if my mother was okay. No one explained anything at the time, and I remember crying, desperate for answers.

Later, I learned that my mother had cut her wrists and tried to take her own life. That moment became one of the most vivid memories of my childhood. At the time, I felt anger toward my stepfather. I held resentment, believing his addiction and infidelity had caused her pain and nearly taken her from us. I recall visiting her at Friends Hospital; she seemed to be back to her normal sober self, just anxious to leave the hospital, stating, "I do want to live, I don't belong here at this hospital," and continuing to apologize to us.

"We are pressed on every side by troubles, but we are not crushed. We are perplexed, but not driven to despair. We are hunted down, but never abandoned by God. We get knocked down, but we are not destroyed." - 2 Corinthians 4:8-9

That experience shaped me in ways I didn't understand then. I learned how to guard my heart, how to block a certain depth of love, believing that loving too deeply could lead to unbearable loss. My trust in men altogether was on a new level of despair. Looking back now, I see God's hand in that moment. It was not her time to leave us, and it was not all on my stepfather. Yet, a combination of continuous hurt and let down. But God protected our family and carried us through a moment that could have changed everything. I believe He intervened and spared us from a loss we were not meant to endure.

"But you, Lord, are a compassionate and gracious God, slow to anger, abounding in love and faithfulness" - Psalm 86:15

Just like with my mother's story, I continued to grow older and even more curious about my stepfather's upbringing. I began to ask questions, slowly piecing together the history that has shaped the man he has become. Believing that learning more about him would help my healing journey and the "why" behind some of these behaviors. I learned that he was introduced to drugs at a very early age and has struggled with addiction for many years.

I didn't grow up with a perfect example of fatherhood, but I did grow up with a man who loved me with the tools he had. I later learned that His father was not active in his life, and I believe that absence shaped much of how he fathered. I have an early memory of meeting his father and siblings. Around that time, they were attempting to connect with him, but by then, addiction had already taken hold. He was deep in his struggles, and it seemed to interfere with his ability to build and maintain healthy relationships.

My stepfather entered fatherhood while still carrying the weight of his own brokenness. As a teenager, he was already entangled in addiction, trying to navigate life with substances that dulled his pain but never healed it. It seems that he did not have the necessary model for healthy parenting or stability to lean on. He was learning as he went, often stumbling, often failing, but still showing up. His love was imperfect and sometimes clouded by his struggles, but it was real. Through him, I learned that love can exist even in the midst of brokenness.

Despite his addiction, I can now tell that my stepfather had a strong desire to protect his family in the only way he knew how. He battled his own demons while still trying to shield us from harm. There were moments when his addiction threatened the very stability he tried to provide, yet his intent to protect never disappeared. That contradiction, brokenness, and protection existing at the same time, taught me that love is not always clean or simple, but it can still be present.

After years of cycling in and out of rehabs, my stepfather eventually found sobriety. His recovery was not just a personal victory; it became a turning point for our family. His clean years stood as proof that redemption is possible, even after decades of struggle. Watching his transformation showed me that addiction does not have to be the final chapter of a person's life. And how we are all important parts of God's perfect plan.

In the end, calling him "Dad" was not about biology or perfection. It was a choice of the heart. He was there from the very beginning, we basically grew up together and the title grew with us. Despite his flaws and the pain his addiction caused, he earned that name through presence and redemption. His love, though imperfect, was passed down, and it shaped my understanding of grace, forgiveness, and God's ability to restore what once seemed broken.

A Prayer for Strength and Love Amid Past Traumas

Heavenly Father,
I come before You with the weight of memories that, at times, can be hard to carry. My heart has been shaped by the brokenness of addiction, by the instability of choices that were not mine, yet still left their mark on me. I confess the hurt, the confusion, and the fear that sometimes rise up when memories from the past start to surface.

Lord, I thank You for the glimpses of care that reminded me I was not forgotten. And I thank You, most of all, for Your protection, which never failed me. Father God, I ask You to heal the places in me that still ache and restore the parts of my heart that were wounded by addiction's shadow.

In this continuous journey of healing, give me the courage to forgive, not to excuse the pain, but to release the hold it may have on me. Give me wisdom to learn from the past without being chained to it.

Today, I celebrate the legacy of sobriety and the testimony that brokenness does not have to be the final word.

In Jesus' Name,
Amen

Chapter

5

A Teen Father's Love Passed Down

Despite the chaos at home, I was fortunate to have my biological father in my life, at least partially at the time. He would pop in from time to time, often unannounced, but always full of energy and joy. Everyone loved him. I did too. To me, he was like sunshine, bright and exciting, but not something I could always count on. When he came around, I'd light up. Even if I had been waiting for hours on the steps with my bag packed, I was still excited each time he actually showed up.

I later came to suspect that substance abuse, along with the weight of becoming a father so young, played a role in his absence. At the time, I was shielded from whatever battles he may have been fighting. Despite her own trauma and addiction, my mother never spoke ill of him. Even when he disappointed me, she protected my heart. She would find gentle ways to explain his absence, giving me space to continue loving him freely, without bitterness. And for that, I will always be grateful.

When I was younger, I had the privilege of spending time with my father's side of the family here and there. Whenever I came around, I was met with warmth, gentleness, and love. As I write this chapter, one memory stands out clearly: a brief period when I moved to South Carolina with my father and one of my aunts. I was still young then, young enough to lose one of my front teeth while I was there, a small but vivid marker of that season of my life.

My aunt was attending college there at the time, and I remember arriving and being completely mesmerized by the ducks that wandered freely around the area. I could feed them myself, and the experience filled me with an overwhelming sense of joy. Life down south felt different from what I was used to in Philadelphia. For the first time, I got a glimpse of what living well could feel like, what safety looked like. Still, even in those small pockets of happiness, there were nights when I missed my mother and my siblings back home.

That year, I attended school in South Carolina. I remember riding the yellow school bus, watching it pick me up in the morning and bring me back in the afternoon. Everything about that life felt calmer, steadier, and unfamiliar in the best way.

The transition back to Philadelphia began with a parental disagreement between my father and me. I had a key to the apartment and had been warned about a little girl who might be mean to me or take my things. I was told that if I had company, I wasn't allowed to let her inside. One afternoon after school, I was playing inside with a friend when that same little girl asked if she could join us. I was just a child, and feeling bad for her, I let her come in.

When my father came home and saw what had happened, he became very upset. He yelled at me, made my company leave, and popped me before sending me to my room. I think that was the first, and only, time he ever truly disciplined me, which probably explains my dramatic response. I cried and screamed that I wanted to go home to my mother. Quite literally, the next morning, I woke up in the backseat of the car as we drove back to Philadelphia.

I was happy to be reunited with my mother and family, but sad to leave behind a better lifestyle. Still, I thank God for allowing me to have those experiences. They shaped my expectations for how I wanted to live and what I wanted to provide for my own children. To this day, I sometimes wonder how life might have turned out if my father had never brought me back to Philadelphia. Then again, I know the God I serve is intentional. I think I turned out just fine, as a matter of fact, my experiences, both great and challenging, helped shape the woman and mother I am today.

"And we know that in all things God works for the good of those who love Him." - Romans 8:28

In the spaces where my father could not always be present, his sisters filled me with something just as powerful. I had four aunts on my father's side whom I deeply looked up to. One of my father's sisters, who has since passed on to be with the Lord, held a particularly special place in my heart. She would often take me to her home and let me stay over with her and my older cousin. She welcomed me in without hesitation. During my teenage years, she would pop up on me, let me do her hair while we talked, and catch up on life. By that time, I was in my early teens and did not see my father often. Almost without fail, she would end up calling him and saying, "Here, someone wants to talk to you," before handing me the phone. Such a sweet soul, always making sure I knew just how loved I was, no matter how much time had passed. All of my father's sisters have always been and are still incredibly special to me. Just knowing I had them felt like a warm blanket of safety I could snuggle into when times were hard.

But still, there were cracks. Deep ones. The absence of my father in the in-between moments, the birthdays he missed, the calls that never came, the silence when I needed protection, left wounds I didn't know how to name until I was older. I didn't realize then how much his absence shaped the way I viewed love, trust, and men. I carried that pain into my own relationships. I looked for pieces of my father in the boys I dated, chasing the thrill of their attention, clinging to the fear of their rejection. I confused inconsistency with passion, and chaos with connection. I was trying to rewrite my story through other people, hoping they would show up for me the way I wished he had.

But in time, I came to understand something deeper about my father, about his pain, his past, and the journey that shaped him. Not too long ago, while working on a genogram project for a class, I separately interviewed each of my parents to learn more about their childhoods. This became more than just a school assignment, but instead, a necessary shift in my journey of healing.

During the conversation with my father, I discovered that my paternal grandfather, too, struggled with alcoholism and was absent for much of my father's early life. Because of his drinking, my grandmother often refused to let him see their children. My father explained how he grew up largely without his father's presence, and in hearing this, I began to see him in a new light, not just as my dad, but as someone who carried his own wounds into teenage fatherhood.

"Just because someone didn't love you the way you needed doesn't mean you're unlovable. It means they were still learning how to love themselves." -Unknown

My father is the baby of six siblings on his mother's side, and next to the youngest of seven on his father's side. He was just nineteen when he lost his mother in a tragic car accident caused by a drunk driver. He was in the car when it happened, on the way down south for a family wedding that would never be the same. I don't remember ever meeting my grandmother and have only seen pictures of her. My aunts often say I remind them of her, especially when they speak of her leadership and resilience.

I was only three years old when he lost her, but I imagine he lost more than just a parent that day. He lost his sense of safety, of direction. He was still a child himself, suddenly forced to face a grief most adults can barely survive. And like so many Black men who were taught to be strong before they were taught to be whole, he numbed the pain the only way he knew how. Substance abuse became a shadow in his life, and over time, I can see how this can affect a young, growing man long-term.

Still, when he did show up for me, he tried. He cracked jokes, danced with me, played music, and made me feel special in the moments we had. Not to mention the amazing cook he is even till this current day! He made our time feel like an adventure. And that mattered, even if it was not always consistent.

"Love bears all things, believes all things, hopes all things, endures all things." - 1 Corinthians 13:7

With that all said, I will not pretend the wounds aren't there, but I also won't pretend he didn't love me. I've learned to hold both truths. I give grace to the version of my father who was lost and hurting, because I've come to know the version of him who has come so far in his own journey and is still healing.

Today, our relationship is one of the greatest gifts in my life. He is like a best friend to me now, someone I can call at any time, about anything. We laugh, we reminisce, we share real conversations. He continues to show up as a father and grandfather in ways he never could before.

Along the way, my father also found love again. His marriage brought a steady, joyful presence into his life, and into mine. My stepmother adds warmth, support, and light in ways I didn't know I needed, and I'm grateful for the role she plays in our family and in the man my father continues to become. I used to grieve what I didn't get from him, but now I celebrate what we've built. I can truly say we grew up together.

This chapter speaks truth to the power of love. And it exemplifies the never-failing love of God. The healing takes time, and together we are still on that journey, but it is so worth it. Because sometimes, broken people still need more grace to grow. Sometimes, they bloom late. And sometimes, if you're lucky, you get to see a better version of them.

A Prayer for the Teen Parent with Father Wounds

Dear God,

I come to You carrying the weight of absence, of unanswered questions, unmet needs, and memories that both ache and glow. You see the part of me that still longs for what I never received. The love was inconsistent. The protection I needed but didn't have. The affection I chased in others, trying to fill a gap I couldn't explain. I ask You now to touch those empty places with Your healing hand.

Help me forgive what was broken, even when it still hurts. Help me see the humanity in those who hurt me, without excusing their choices, but without letting bitterness rule my heart.

Lord, give me the strength to parent from a place of healing, not pain. Let the cycle end with me. Let my children experience a love that is steady, present, and whole. When I feel alone in this journey, remind me that You are the Father who never leaves, but the One who always shows up. Thank You for the grace that covers me, and the future that still holds joy, no matter how my story began.

In Jesus' name I pray,
Amen

Chapter

6

Innocence Interrupted

Before I understood love, I learned absence. Before I understood safety, I learned instability. As you have read, the men who were meant to anchor my life were either missing or consumed by their own battles, and my mother was fighting demons of her own. These early fractures quietly shaped how I sought connection, how I interpreted attention, and how I measured my worth. I was a little girl seeking family, love, and belonging. We moved often, and I longed for stability, for a healthy environment that felt secure. I clung to neighbors and to the few people I believed were safe and kind.

But there is a deeper memory, one that predates my awareness of boys, men, or relationships altogether. It is a truth I avoided for years, yet it holds the key to understanding the roots of my fear, my resilience, and my becoming.

I cannot remember my exact age, only that I was younger than ten, still a little girl who trusted the world around her. During that season of my life, I spent a great deal of time with my neighbors and their extended family. I was often invited to tag along to their relatives' homes, and sometimes I stayed overnight.

One of those nights remains etched in my memory, not because of joy or childhood adventure, but because it marked the moment something inside me shifted. We were sleeping on the living room floor, my friend, a few of her cousins, and I. The house was full, the kind of place where people laughed loudly, talked freely, and moved about without much structure. I remember falling asleep feeling safe enough, surrounded by other children.

Sometime in the night, I woke to the sensation of someone touching me. The room was dark, and I kept my eyes closed, pretending to be asleep while silently praying that nothing more would happen. I could tell the person was an adult male. I didn't know who he was, my friend's uncle, one of the older cousins, or someone else entirely, but I knew he was grown, and I knew what he was doing was wrong.

I stayed still, terrified, hoping my stillness would make him stop touching me underneath my underwear and rubbing his hands, skin to skin, across my underdeveloped breast. As things progressed, I could feel him putting his fingers into my private area. When I shifted my body, I heard him whisper, *Shhhh*. That sound still echoes in my memory.

This must have gone on for more than ten minutes, which felt like a lifetime for me. I kept moving until he finally got up and walked away. Only then did I open my eyes. My shirt lifted to my neck, and my underwear had been pulled down to my knees. I fixed my clothing with shaking hands and cried silently, afraid to make a sound, afraid to wake anyone, afraid he would return, afraid to be seen.

"He healeth the broken in heart, and bindeth up their wounds." - Psalm 147:3

I stayed awake until the first light of morning crept through the window. When the house came alive with laughter and conversation, I felt numb. No energy to play with the other children, no appetite to eat breakfast. All I wanted was to go home. This was when my innocence was interrupted, quietly and without warning, marking the beginning of a journey I would spend many years learning how to understand and reclaim.

I couldn't look any of the men in the face. I didn't know who had violated my trust, but I knew something precious had been taken. I also didn't know then that it wasn't my fault. Today, as

I process this truth, I understand clearly: it was never my fault. Adults are meant to protect children, not harm them.

Writing these words in this chapter is the first time I have ever spoken about that night. So I thank you, my readers, for processing this truth with me. For years, I buried it so deeply that I convinced myself forgetting was the only way to survive, and that forgetting was the same as healing. But trauma does not disappear simply because we refuse to look at it. It waits. However, healing required me to stop running, to return to the memory, to face the fear, and to reclaim the little girl who did not deserve what happened to her.

"Forgiveness is not an occasional act; it is a constant attitude."- Martin Luther King Jr.

Today, despite the long-term pain his actions caused, I choose forgiveness. Not because what happened was acceptable, but because I refuse to let that moment define the rest of my life. I forgive the man who harmed me and violated my trust, whoever he was. And I forgive myself for the years I spent believing I should have done something differently.

There was nothing I could have done. I was just a little girl trying to belong, hoping to be accepted. My innocence was taken without my consent, but right now, on this day, my voice, my healing, and my truth are mine to reclaim! So, I speak now to the little girl inside me and tell her the truth: *It was not your fault. You did nothing to deserve this. You were a child, and you were worthy of protection.*

This experience matters in my story because it explains so much of what came after. It is part of my "why", the why behind my fears, my boundaries or lack thereof, my silence, and eventually, my strength. Writing this is not about reopening wounds, but about closing them properly.

I hope you, as my readers, understand how sharing this now is an important part of my healing journey. And I hope that someone else, carrying their own childhood wounds, will find courage in my honesty to one day proclaim freedom in their own truth. If my story gives even one person the courage to face their past with compassion, forgiveness, and grace, then this chapter serves a purpose far beyond my own healing.

A Prayer for the Wounded Reader

Lord God,
I come to you right now for the one who needed to pause, breathe, or wipe away tears after this last chapter. Father, you are the God of comfort and compassion,

I lift the reader who has come to this place carrying memories that are heavy and tender. You see what others may not see. You know the wounds that words can stir and the pain that silence once held. Wrap them now in Your peace.

For the one who was harmed as a child, remind them gently that it was never their fault. Speak truth louder than shame. Restore what was taken and soothe what still aches. Where fear learned to live, plant safety. For the one who feels triggered, overwhelmed, or unsteady, slow their breathing and steady their heart.

Father God, help them feel grounded in Your presence. Let them know they are not alone, and that healing does not have to be rushed.. Lord God, on this day, cover every reader with gentleness. Restore their rest and renew their strength.

In the mighty name of Jesus I pray,
Amen

Chapter

7

Guilt and Shame of Teen Sex

As I grew older and experienced so much during my earlier years, the love I had known at home was no longer enough to fill the growing gaps inside me. During my teenage years, my relationship with my mother became increasingly strained due to her substance use. We didn't communicate well. Arguments became common, and I can admit there were times I responded with disrespect. The weight of her being under the influence pressed heavily on me, creating a distance between us that neither of us truly knew how to bridge. It wasn't until she found her way into sobriety that healing began. In those years of clarity, we were able to mend what had been broken and rebuild a bond that became stronger than it had ever been.

Nevertheless, the pain, the silence, and the deep longing for connection had once led me down paths I didn't fully understand. But my story isn't only about surviving the brokenness; it's also about the choices I made in the aftermath, and how they shaped the journey that followed.

No one really talked to me about sex. As mentioned in the chapter before, the introduction was secret and inappropriate. So, I learned other layers of the act the hard way.

I don't say that to be dramatic. I say it because it's the truth. Growing up, there weren't many open conversations at home about relationships, love, or protecting myself. Nobody pulled me aside to break down what sex really meant, not just physically, but emotionally. I was left to figure it out on my own, and like most teenagers, curiosity didn't wait for permission.

I experienced sex for the first time at an early age, too early. And now that I look back, I can say it wasn't just curiosity that led me there. I was searching for something. I wanted to fit in with the cool crowd. I wanted to feel seen. I wanted to feel valued. I was trying to fill an emotional space that I didn't have the language for at the time. That space was made of all the things I felt like I was missing, such as attention, safety, love, and understanding.

Although leadership seemed to be the theme and expectation in my life, there were times in childhood when I chose to be a follower. I became curious at a very young age, and because I was quiet and "mature," I believe teen sex was the last thing my mother thought I would be doing.

Looking for love in all the wrong places, I made immature decisions that reflected the confusion I felt inside. When I reflect on those moments, I see a little girl who felt broken, as if something vital was missing. I was trying to find my place in this big world, reaching for connection and meaning in places that could never truly satisfy. What I didn't realize back then was that what I needed most was to seek God.

"You will seek me and find me when you seek me with all your heart." - Jeremiah 29:13

I was never one of the popular kids, but I wanted, desperately, to belong. I was a straight-A student, the kind of student teachers relied on, and I noticed that the friends I did have often came around when they needed homework answers or help studying. Still, being included in any way felt better than being invisible.

By eighth grade, I started spending more time with a small group of friends from school, hanging out after classes let out. It was during one of those after-school gatherings that things began to shift. There was a boy there who embodied many of the personality traits I didn't have: outgoing, confident, well-liked, and looking back now, I realize I had a quiet crush on him. I admired his boldness, the ease with which he moved through the world, and I longed to feel that same sense of acceptance from others.

That day, with him, I made a choice I didn't fully understand at the time. Wanting to fit in and wanting his attention more than I wanted to listen to my own instincts, I followed along. We were still children, though we didn't see it that way then, crossing into things meant for adults, trying to feel grown without grasping the consequences that could follow.

Nobody talked to me about birth control. No one explained how to protect myself from STDs, pregnancy, or the emotional weight that comes with being intimate before you're ready. In my world, sex wasn't part of a healthy conversation; it was hidden, ignored, or taboo and treated like something you just figured out in secret.
So that's exactly what I did. In secret.

I found out I was pregnant during the summer before my ninth-grade year. Initially, I ignored it and didn't know what was happening in my body until I started to feel the small flutter that felt like gas bubbles and realized it was a human growing inside of me. I kept it to myself, terrified, ashamed, and in complete denial. I didn't say a word to anyone. I carried that pregnancy in silence for months, hiding my growing body under baggy clothes and avoiding situations where someone might notice.

For those first several months in secrecy, I had no prenatal care. No doctor's visits. No vitamins. I didn't know what was happening inside my body, and to be honest, I was scared to know. I lived every day hoping no one would notice, praying that somehow this would all go away or that I would magically wake up from what felt like a very real nightmare.

It wasn't until I was about six months along that my mother found out. And even then, it wasn't because I told her. It was because she realized something was off; our cycle was usually on the same week, and she finally noticed I hadn't been using pads. She started asking questions, putting the pieces together. And once the truth came out, everything changed.

Once word spread, so did the opinions. I was told we were both too young, that I still had growing up to do, that this was a mistake that could be undone. An abortion was offered to me, all expenses paid. I was warned about how risky terminating this late in the pregnancy was and even told that I could die in the process. The message was clear: this was something I should not continue. And I was only given a few days to decide.

So young I was, with so many thoughts running through my head. I had already been carrying life inside of me for six months, and there was no denying that. I had felt the fluttering, the movement, the quiet reminders that I was no longer alone.

There was no way I could end it. I had already grown attached to my child, already formed a bond I couldn't explain but deeply felt. Even though I was still a scared child myself, I made a promise to my unborn baby and to myself that I would do everything I could to be there. Even if I had to do it alone.

That summer, the one that should have been full of sleepovers, mall trips, and teenage memories, was filled with guilt, isolation, and fear. I honestly didn't know who I was anymore. I didn't feel like a child, but I didn't feel ready to be a mother either. And as the school year crept closer, so did the shame. A cloud of depression hovered over me. I slept most of my days away, praying for refuge. Even then, God was oh so present, providing a safe place to lay my shame and burdens.

"Shame dies when stories are told in safe places." – Ann Voskamp

I ended up missing most of my ninth-grade year at Dobbins Randolph High School and was told I would have to repeat the 9th grade. The absenteeism wasn't because I hated school. I actually loved school; it was where I felt the safest. I just didn't want to continue with the embarrassment and shame. Walking into that school pregnant was shameful enough. I didn't want the continued stares. I didn't want continued whispers. I didn't want to have to answer questions I didn't have the strength or words for. So, I miraculously got sick every time I stood at the bus stop on my way to school. After a few of those scares, I was able to stay home. And the silence that started as protection turned into a prison.

Looking back, that season of my life was marked by guilt and shame, emotions far heavier than any child should have to carry. Pregnant, at the fragile age of fourteen, I had to be brave and resilient, not just for myself, but for the life growing inside of me. Although my mother did not force me to end the pregnancy, the decision was placed entirely in my hands, and I was asked to make a choice far bigger than my age or maturity could fully comprehend.

In the moments leading to my decision, I was forced to grow up quickly, navigating adulthood while still a child myself. The love I had known up to that point was often inconsistent and dysfunctional, and the shame surrounding teen sex only deepened the weight I carried on my shoulders. Yet even in my fear and confusion, something within me chose protection, responsibility, and love. The choice was made, I chose life over death, I chose to protect my unborn child even through the fear of what the future would hold. And that choice, made in the midst of guilt and uncertainty, shifted me to the next level. It, among other things, became the beginning of my resilience.

Prayer For Healing from Dysfunctional Love

Lord,
Thank You for seeing the parts of my story that no one else did. Thank You for the protection that came even in the midst of chaos.

Help me to heal from the love that hurt me, and hold on to the love that sustained me. Teach me to separate pain from purpose, and to walk forward with a heart that is whole, even if it's still healing. Give me wisdom to love better, and grace for those who didn't know how to love me the way I needed.

Even when I feel the pull of old habits, remind me I am not who I used to be. You are renewing my mind,
Restoring my heart, And rewriting my story with grace.

Thank you for showing me that being "chosen" doesn't mean being perfect; It means being willing. Willing to face the hard things. Willing to heal. Willing to believe that change is possible through You. Thank You for being the constant when people couldn't be. Thank You, Oh Lord, for never leaving me.

In the mighty name of Jesus,
Amen

Chapter

8

Unwrapping My New Reality

It was Christmas Eve 1998. At this stage of the pregnancy, I was wabbling around with what looked like a basketball under my shirt. I went in for what I thought was just a routine check-up. I wasn't in any real pain, just some light cramps and a little lower back discomfort. So when the doctor examined me and casually said, "You're already five centimeters dilated," I blinked at her, confused. I had no idea what that meant. I wasn't scared, not yet, just unsure. Still so young, still so unaware of what was about to happen.

They had me change into a gown and told me I'd be having my baby that night. While most teenagers were unwrapping gifts and planning outfits for holiday dinners, I was lying in a hospital bed, unwrapping my new reality. I wasn't thinking about presents under a tree. I was thinking about contractions, baby names, and the life I was about to bring into the world, a life that would change mine forever.

Just like that. I remember lying in a hospital bed, listening to the sounds of other women down the hallway, screaming, crying, laboring loudly. I was quiet. I felt like I was floating in and out of disbelief, unsure what emotions were even mine. Was I afraid? Excited? In shock? Probably all three. Mostly, I remember feeling lost. I had no birth plan, no idea what to expect, and no real understanding of what it meant to deliver a child. Still, wondering how this huge thing was going to come out of me. I just did what they told me. I followed the instructions, step by step, because I didn't know what else to do besides be strong.

"Be strong and courageous. Do not be afraid; do not be discouraged, for the Lord your God will be with you wherever you go." – Joshua 1:9

There was no epidural, no heavy pain medications, just me and the growing intensity of labor. When they checked again and said I was 10 centimeters and ready to push, they turned on big lights all around me. About five doctors entered the room with masks and gloves on, preparing for the arrival. I braced myself, still unsure of how this "big thing" was supposed to come out of me.

But somehow, in just two and a half pushes, it happened. He

came flying into the world so fast the doctor couldn't catch him, but my mother did. True story. My son shot out with such force that my mom caught him in her hands like a miracle she wasn't expecting. She still tells that story to this day, how she caught her first grandson before anyone else could. My son was born weighing eight pounds, and the moment they placed him on me, skin to skin, everything felt both still and overwhelming at the same time.

After the room settled and the nurses cleaned him up, they brought him to me and placed him back in my arms. He was so small. His skin still a little wrinkled, his cries soft but certain. I stared down at this tiny person, my son, and in that moment, everything around me faded into a blur. It was surreal. I was 14 years old. Fourteen. Holding a baby I had grown inside of me. A real-life baby.

"Sometimes the smallest things take up the most room in your heart." - A.A. Milne

If I can be honest, I didn't feel like a mother right away. I felt overwhelmed. My body ached, my mind raced, and my heart was full, but also heavy. I was exhausted, scared, and somehow still numb. Part of me wanted to cry, but I didn't know which tears were for joy and which were for fear.
I remember thinking, *What now?*
How was I supposed to take care of a whole human being when

I still needed so much care myself?

There was love, real, deep, immediate love. But also panic. I worried I wasn't enough. That I would mess it all up. I felt guilt for bringing him into a world I wasn't fully prepared for, and shame for being "that girl" a statistic, a stereotype, a child raising a child.

But beneath all that, there was also a quiet strength beginning to rise. I had no idea how, but I knew I would figure it out. I had to. Because he was mine, and from the moment I held him, I knew he deserved everything I never had. It was sacred, surreal, and terrifying. I remember looking at his tiny fingers and full cheeks, wondering how someone so small could carry such a big piece of my heart. I was a teenager, still learning how to take care of myself, but now I was someone's mother. And in that moment, nothing else mattered.

A Prayer for the Teen Parent Waiting to Give Birth

Dear God,

I'm scared. I don't know exactly what to expect, and honestly, sometimes I don't even know how to feel. One minute I'm excited, and the next I'm overwhelmed by the pain, the responsibility, the unknowns.

This baby inside me is real, and soon they'll be here, looking to me for everything. And I don't always feel ready. I'm still growing up myself. But Lord, I believe that You don't make mistakes.

If You allowed this life to grow inside of me, then You must believe I have what it takes. Even when I doubt myself, remind me that You don't doubt me. Cover me with peace when fear creeps in. Be in the room with me when labor begins.

Give me strength, breath by breath, contraction by contraction. Help me trust my body, and trust that You will carry me through. And when the moment comes, when I hold my baby for the first time. Lord, let me feel the kind of love that silences fear.

In Jesus' name I pray,
Amen

Chapter

9

He's Here: Now What?

The day my firstborn son arrived, everything changed. It wasn't just the birth of a baby; it was the birth of a new version of me. One who had no choice but to grow up quickly. One that had to learn love, patience, sacrifice, and strength in real time.

While other teenagers were unwrapping gifts that Christmas Eve, I was unwrapping a brand-new life, one I didn't feel ready for, but one I knew I had to face head-on. Fear and shame crept up, but I would not allow that to be my portion. I had God to look to for strength.

"Those who look to Him are radiant; their faces are never covered with shame." - Psalm 34:5

This verse is a reminder that shame doesn't have the final say.

No matter what you've been through, when you lift your eyes to God, He sees you as whole, worthy, and loved.

There were no flashing cameras or proud school announcements. No balloons. No flowers. Just me, my son, and a silence filled with emotions I couldn't even name. Exhaustion. Awe. Fear. Love. Grief for the childhood I was leaving behind. Hope for the life I was holding in my hands.

I spent my Christmas in the hospital that year, shuffling through baby name options most of the day. I wanted his name to mean something. I wanted it to speak to strength and purpose. Because even though I didn't feel strong at that moment, I knew that being his mother would give me a reason to find strength every single day.

When I left the hospital, I didn't just walk out with a newborn. I walked out with a new identity. But the world outside didn't pause to let me adjust. Life kept going, and school was waiting.

A few months after my son was born, I had no choice but to return to the reality of my teenage life. Around that time, we had moved yet again and had a new neighborhood school. I got transferred to Edison Ferrera High School. It was supposed to be a fresh start, a clean slate.

Walking through those new hallways felt heavy. I carried more than just a backpack. I carried the weight of being a teen mom. The fear of being judged. The pressure to succeed while still figuring out who I was. I wasn't very popular and could count the few friends I had on one hand. Still, I showed up. With a heavy heart, I walked into that new beginning, unsure of what was ahead but knowing I couldn't go backward.

"It does not matter how slowly you go as long as you do not stop." – Confucius

And that's what this chapter of my life taught me: shame grows in silence, but healing begins the moment we speak. Returning to school was harder than I ever imagined. I transferred to a new high school to avoid the judgment and whispers I feared would follow me if I went back to the old one. On the outside, it may have looked like a fresh start, but on the inside, I was still carrying the weight of my new life, physically, emotionally, and spiritually.

I remember standing in the hallway those first few days, surrounded by the echoes of students' laughter, as they socialized with joy about weekend plans and boy crushes. Meanwhile, I was worrying about my son getting a diaper rash, his bottle schedules, and whether or not I'd be able to get enough rest for the next day due to midnight feedings.

I didn't fit in. I didn't feel seen. I was a mother, in a kid's body, in a room full of kids. And the hardest part? Leaving my son every morning. No one prepares you for the way your heart rips a little when you walk away from your baby. The tears I held back in the school bathroom weren't about classes or grades. They were about missing my little one, wondering if he missed me too.

Overall, I felt like I was failing in both worlds: not enough of a teen to fit in, not enough of an adult to figure it all out. But I kept going.

Even through the exhaustion, even through the fear, even through the nights when I questioned everything, I still showed up. Because he needed me. And even more than that, I realized…I needed him too. He gave my life direction. A reason to hope. A reason to be better.

My firstborn son became my anchor in a season when I could have drifted into depression, resentment, or regret. There were storms- emotional ones, spiritual ones, and financial ones- but he kept me grounded. He reminded me that even though my life took a turn I didn't plan for, it was still a life worth fighting for.

Yes, I missed out on some things, such as school dances, house parties, and even carefree weekends. But I gained something deeper. I gained perspective. Purpose. And a kind of love that has no conditions and no expiration date. Becoming a mother didn't ruin my life. It revealed it.

"Would I ever bring this nation to the point of birth and then not deliver it?" asks the Lord. "No! I would never keep this nation from being born," says your God. - Isaiah 66:9

Just remember, God didn't bring you this far to abandon you now. The birth of your child is not the end of your story, but the beginning of your strength. The verse continues to remind us of God's sovereignty and His divine control over all aspects of creation.

Thelma R. Davis-Clanton

A Prayer of Gratitude

Father God,
I come before You with a tender heart, full of memories that still feel close, even though years have passed.

Thank You for being present with me on the day my firstborn son entered this world. Thank You for meeting me in that hospital room, in the quiet of Christmas Eve, when fear and shame tried to wrap themselves around my heart.

Even then, Lord, You whispered strength.
Even then, Lord, You called me radiant when I felt anything but.
Even then, Lord, You saw a mother where I only saw a scared little girl.

Father God, today, I thank You for giving me the courage to step into a season I didn't feel ready for. Thank You for teaching me love in real time, for stretching my capacity beyond my years, and for wrapping me in grace when exhaustion, doubt, and loneliness threatened to break me.

You provided new mercies every day. You never let shame have the final say. You covered me with dignity, purpose, and resilience. I love you so much Lord, I truly, truly do!

Amen

Before I close this chapter, I thought it would be nice to share a poem I wrote in 2019 and read to my oldest son at his 21st birthday party. A poem from a mother's heart to her firstborn, my Day One:

My Day One

The number 1 means first
It's like waking up to the morning sun.
The first one to call me "Mom"?
Yup, that be you,
My Day One.

You were the beginning of my maturity.
We learned and grew up together.
On punishment together, we still had fun
Yup, that be you,
My Day One.

The saying goes, "ride till the wheels fall off"
And that you always do!
Through all my ups and downs,
When I thought I had no one,
You were right there.
Yup, that be you,
My Day One.

Always there to wipe my tears away.
Always there to say, "Mommy, it will be okay."
A son a mother could have only dreamed of,
Yup, that be you,
My Day One.

Your craft and talents are amazing.
You are a blessing to those around you.
You are dope and inspiring to me, son
Yeah, you,
My Day One.

As a family, no matter what comes our way,
When it's all said and done,
We know we have you to look forward to
My son-son.
Yup, that be you
Ty-Queal N. Davis, My Day One

Chapter

10

Looking for Love in All the Wrong Places

As the months and years passed, I started noticing things about myself, little reactions, fears, and habits that didn't come from teen motherhood itself, but from the little girl inside me who still needed healing. Becoming a young parent didn't erase my past; if anything, it shines a light on the parts I've tried to ignore. I began to see the patterns I inherited, the wounds I never tended to, and the ways my unmet needs were quietly shaping the way I loved, protected, and made decisions.

Working to do my best and my determination to succeed as a teen mother juggling life, I found myself still looking for love in all the wrong places. Becoming a teen mother didn't stop my childhood wounds from bleeding. It didn't erase the insecurities or silences I had learned to live with. And even though I was determined to do right by my son, I still found myself searching for love in places that could never give it to me. In hindsight, I can see that much of what I called "choices" were really cries for attention, affection, and belonging. But at the time, all I knew was that something inside me felt empty, and I kept trying to fill it. Even then, I had so much growing up to still do.

People might wonder how a fifteen-year-old with a baby even had time to think about boys, sex, or relationships. But that's the thing about unhealed wounds: they don't care about your responsibilities. They show up anyway. I didn't have the words for it back then, but now I understand. I was trying to fill a father-shaped void with the attention of boys who were never meant to carry that role. It wasn't about love. It was about longing. About emptiness. It was about wanting to be seen, chosen, and valued.

Transparent moment, *so please don't judge me!*
It's a memory that comes to mind as I process this chapter of my memoir:

There was a boy who lived up the block from me, a boy my mother did not want me dealing with. My son was a toddler at the time, and I assume she was trying to protect me in her own way. She warned me over and over again, but something in me did the opposite of everything she said. Not because I wanted trouble, but because I was a walking cry for help. A wounded little girl, a mother, in a teenage body, seeking validation in all the wrong ways.

I started sneaking around with him behind her back. We were young, reckless, and clueless. I still can't remember whose idea it was, but he started climbing a ladder to my bedroom window at night, tapping gently until I opened it. One night, my mother must have heard a noise and came to check. We hid under the covers, pretending to sleep, but when she flipped the light on, she saw four feet at the bottom of the bed. Four feet, two of mine, two of his, and in an instant, IT GOT REAL!

She ripped the blanket off us, yelling and cursing as she swung that broom like a weapon of disappointment. She chased him down the stairs and out the front door with nothing but his socks on, then came right back up and swung at me next as I danced around that room, running from the broom. That's a beating I brought on myself. She was furious, and honestly, at that time, I didn't have an answer for her. Not one that made sense. I didn't fully understand myself or why I kept putting my heart and body in places that could only break me more. Even when I didn't feel loved or safe, God's everlasting love was already surrounding me.

"I have loved you with an everlasting love." – Jeremiah 31:3

That truth of God's love didn't change my circumstances overnight, but it planted a seed of hope that would carry me through some of my darkest choices. I finally decided to leave the boy alone. Maybe a little too late. Just a few weeks later, following the embarrassing broom beating, I started to feel sick and noticed my cycle was only on for 1 day. I remember it being shortly after my 16th birthday, I took a pregnancy test and found out I was pregnant with my second child.

I was terrified. Even though my mother battled her own struggles with addiction, she didn't play when it came to discipline. The icing on the cake, she warned me over and over about that boy. The thought of telling her made me nauseous, sick to my stomach. I remember calling my stepfather while I stood in the bathroom, holding the positive test with tears in my eyes. "Dad... you're gonna be mad at me," I whispered.
He looked at me and said, "Don't tell me you're pregnant again."

The silence between us said everything. He was the first one I told, mostly because I felt safe sharing it with him. On the other hand, I needed someone who wouldn't kill me on sight. I asked him to help me break the news to my mother, maybe a family meeting with my siblings there too, hoping that would soften the blow.

Later that night, he gathered us in the living room for a family meeting. She looked at me with a stare that could burn straight through bone. It was like she already knew something was up.

What do you need to tell me? she asked, her voice low and dangerous.

I could barely make eye contact. I broke down crying. She already knew. Her disappointment hung in the air like smoke. The entire house went still, a dry quiet. She finally said, *if you're having another baby, you're moving out with the father. Another baby is not coming into this house.* After that, I ran off to bed, in tears, ashamed and disappointed, just hoping to sleep away some of my heartache.

A few days later, I went to the doctor and discovered I was already three months pregnant with a baby girl. When I returned home and showed her the ultrasound, something softened. She hugged me and simply said, "I guess we have another baby coming." Her love was complicated, but it was still love.

Looking back now, I understand why this memory hits so deeply. I wasn't just being rebellious. I was unhealed. I was longing. I was hurting. And I tried to soothe that hurt with intimacy, attention, and touch. I've had to go back and forgive myself for that. The younger me didn't know how to cope. She acted from emptiness, not wisdom. She responded from a place of pain, not purpose.

"You have searched me, Lord, and You know me." – Psalm 139:1

Even when I didn't know who I was, God did. He saw the hurting girl beneath the rebellion, the longing behind my choices, and the child trying to survive in a world that demanded more than she knew how to give.

Almost immediately, the situation with that boy faded away once everyone learned I was pregnant again. That second pregnancy was different; I knew I couldn't afford another setback. I was always told I was creative, multitalented, and good with my hands. So, I put those talents to work.

I started braiding hair at a local barbershop and doing hair on the side to make money. I needed independence, financially, emotionally, and mentally. And without even realizing it, those early responsibilities taught me something valuable: how to save, plan, and think ahead. While other teenagers were thinking about parties and clothes, I was learning budgeting, discipline, and how to stretch a dollar. It felt like survival. It was my pathway to stability.

Reflecting now, I didn't realize how the same strategies I relied on as a teenager would become the foundation of my financial stability in later adulthood. God's grace was sufficient, and He saw to it that I had the strength to grow in independence and resilience, long before I understood why I needed those lessons.

"My grace is sufficient for you, for My power is made perfect in weakness." – 2 Corinthians 12:9

My daughter was born in September, and by then, my son was almost two years old. Around that time, I didn't understand how deeply I depended on God's grace. How he truly carried me through. But looking back now, I can see it clearly. His strength showed up in every moment when mine fell short.

A Prayer for the Heart That Chased Validation

Dear Heavenly Father,
I come before You with a heart that remembers where I've been and a spirit that longs to grow into who You are shaping me to become.

Lord, I thank You for seeing me even when I didn't know how to see myself. Thank You for loving me through my confusion, my wounds, my longing, and my search for identity.

You were there in every decision, every mistake, and every moment I tried to fill my emptiness with things that were never meant to satisfy me.

Father, I lift up the younger version of me, the girl who wanted affection, the girl who wanted to be noticed, the girl who tried to make sense of her pain the only way she knew how.

Lord God, wrap her in Your compassion. Replace her fears with fresh faith and her worries with strength and courage. Continue Your healing work in her, Oh Lord, until every hidden place shines with Your light.

Father, cover her in Your grace. Teach me how to continue forgiving her and loving her with the same tenderness You show me daily.

Lord, heal every place in me that was shaped by absenteeism and broken love. Heal the wounds that made me seek validation in the wrong places. Heal the insecurities that whispered lies to my heart. Let Your truth silence every false belief I carried about my worth. I surrender every regret to You Oh Lord.

In Jesus' name I pray,
Amen.

Chapter

11

A Vow to My Three Stoogents

A few years after having my second child, my life was already demanding more from me than I felt I had to give. I was juggling single motherhood and a heavy work schedule, fresh out of high school, and working long shifts at a daycare while also doing hair on the side.

At the same time, my mother and stepfather were still deeply caught in the grip of addiction, and my biological father drifted in and out of my life with years of no contact in between. Everything felt full, heavy, and stretched thin, even as I tried to hold it all together.

Somewhere in the middle of that exhaustion, I became involved with another guy. We were together for about two years while I was still living with my mother. I still struggle to find the words to explain how that relationship unfolded. It wasn't always healthy, though at the time I couldn't see how much worse it would become. In the beginning, especially while raising two small children, it just felt like companionship: someone to help share the weight of everyday life.

I remember the exact day I found out I was pregnant again. Yup, baby number three all before I was twenty-one. I was at work, at the daycare, not feeling quite like myself. Another staff member wasn't feeling well either. She was a few years older than me, married, and she and her husband had been trying for a baby for quite some time. Half-joking, half-hopeful, she went to the store and bought pregnancy tests for the both of us.

I laughed and told her, *Girl, don't waste your money. I'm not pregnant.*

Later that afternoon, we went into separate bathrooms to take the tests. A few minutes passed, and then we both came out, crying. She was in tears because her test was negative. I was in tears because mine was positive.

In that moment, joy and fear collided. I felt shock, guilt, disbelief, and responsibility all at once. I was carrying a life I hadn't planned for, while standing next to a woman who wanted nothing more than what I had just discovered.

"Life is not about waiting for the storm to pass, but about

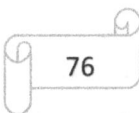

learning how to dance in the rain." - Vivian Greene

I would go on to be in a relationship with my third child's father for nearly six years. That relationship would later become a story of its own, one I speak more deeply about in the next book of this series, but here, it matters because a life came from it.

Eventually, in spite of the red flags in the relationship, after saving every dollar I could, the two of us moved in together. On the surface, it looked like the next step toward stability, a fresh start for my little family. But beneath that surface were cracks I didn't yet have the maturity or the healing to recognize. The relationship I hoped would bring peace slowly revealed itself to be something very different, something I would later have to confront and survive.

Not even a year after moving out of my mother's house, with my children then six and four years old, I found myself giving birth yet again. When my third child came into the picture, she completed what I now call my first batch of children, all born before I turned twenty-one.
Those are my older three. *My Three Stooges.*

When I look back at those years, I see a girl searching for love in all the wrong places because she didn't yet know how to find it within herself. I see a young mother trying to fill the emptiness with people who were never meant to heal her wounds. I see my daddy issues for what they were, not an excuse, but an explanation.

I've learned, through my own journey of life, that when you don't heal your childhood, it follows you into every relationship, every decision, and every version of yourself you try to become.

However, something shifted as my children grew. Quietly and deeply, I made a vow, a promise I held close to my heart:

-My kids will not experience what I did.
-They will have a childhood.
-They will have a stable home to grow up in.
-They will grow at the pace children are meant to grow.
-They will not carry burdens meant for adults.
-They will not be placed in the middle of adult co-parenting drama.
-I will protect their innocence with the help of my Lord and Savior.

And I meant every word of that vow.

"I will give you a new heart and put a new spirit in you." - Ezekiel 36:26

But a new life requires a new heart, and I didn't yet realize that

God wanted to heal what I was still hiding. Wanting better for my children was only the first step. Letting Him transform me would require a level of surrender I wasn't prepared for yet.

Without healing, the pain I never faced began shaping how I loved my children, how I protected them, and how I projected my fears onto them. I wanted so badly to spare them from my past, but sometimes the very thing you're running from is the same thing you unknowingly pass on. That was the moment my journey took a turn I never expected, when I realized I wasn't just raising children. I was once again fighting generational patterns I didn't even know were waiting behind the next door.

A Prayer for Unexpected Seasons

Lord,
You are the God who sees what we never planned and walks with us through what we never expected.
I pray for those who found themselves surprised by life, caught off guard by a diagnosis, a pregnancy, a responsibility, or a season they didn't prepare for.

Father God, give peace where fear tries to settle. Give wisdom where confusion lingers. Give courage to those carrying difficult decisions while still caring for others. Help them trust that even when the timing feels wrong, Your presence is right. That even when the path feels uncertain, You are still ordering their steps.

For every heart holding mixed emotions, those of joy and grief, or hope and fear, God, I ask that You bring comfort and clarity. Remind them that nothing surprises You, and nothing about their story is wasted. May You get the glory for every chapter, even the unexpected ones; they can all be used for growth, purpose, and testimony. Wrap them in grace. Strengthen them for the days ahead. And remind them that they are never alone.

In Jesus name,
Amen

Chapter

12

The Growing Pains of Leadership

In my professional life, before anyone knew the weight I was carrying, they knew me as the woman who showed up every day for other people's children.

As mentioned in an earlier chapter, I stepped into the world of early childhood education straight out of high school, and it quickly became more than a job; it became my calling. I started as a toddler teacher, spending my days on tiny chairs, wiping tears, teaching first words, and celebrating small victories that meant everything.

My favorite moments were decorating my classroom and the hallways for the holidays, turning ordinary spaces into places that felt safe, warm, and alive. What began as simply maintaining a clean, organized classroom and following a solid lesson plan slowly expanded. I found myself helping in the office, covering ratios, assisting with paperwork, without realizing I was being prepared for the next season of my life in childcare.

"If your actions inspire others to dream more, learn more, do more, and become more, you are a leader." - John Quincy Adams

Over the years, I grew with the work. I moved from the classroom into leadership, promoted to assistant director, then director, and eventually area business director, overseeing multiple facilities. Most of the staff I supervised were old enough to be my grandmother, and those early stages of leadership had their own growing pains. Earning respect and trust was a challenge.

Many of my staff assumed I was much older than I actually was. I wasn't sure if it was my serious, business-focused nature or the fact that I was juggling my own young children while working a full-time, demanding job.

I remember one staff meeting when birthdays came up, and everyone started guessing my age. I was barely in my early twenties. As the guesses went around the room, they were more than a decade off. I struggled not to be offended.
How in the world?

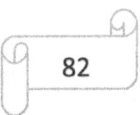

I thought. *Do I really look that old?*

Now I understand, it had little to do with my appearance and everything to do with the weight I carried. Life was never a game for me. Motherhood came early, and with it came responsibility, urgency, and a seriousness that showed up in every room I entered. Many days, I found myself being not just a leader, but a mother figure and counselor to staff and parents alike, simply trying to keep them encouraged. Even then, God was working in me and through me, in the middle of the storm, never leaving my side.

"The Lord himself goes before you and will be with you; he will never leave you nor forsake you." - Deuteronomy 31:8

All of this was happening while I was still navigating the struggles of being a young mother at home. Work became my second home. My staff grew closer to me than some blood relatives, and the children and families I served gave me purpose when my personal life felt anything but stable.

When I clocked into that building, I left my stress, my worries, and my unhealthy relationship chaos at the time clock. To them, I was strong, dependable, and grounded. They never saw the battles I was fighting behind closed doors.

Instead of showing up broken, I used what strength I had left to further my education. During those early years in childcare, I began my college journey at the Community College of Philadelphia, majoring in Early Childhood Education. Those first years at CCP were some of the hardest. Juggling motherhood, the toxic relationship that awaited me at home, the demands of my work, and the tons of coursework each taught me discipline, endurance, sacrifice, and time management. I learned how to keep going even when I was tired, even when quitting would have been easier.

I remember graduating from CCP and my father throwing me a small graduation celebration at his house. During his speech, he told me how proud he was of the mother and the woman I was becoming. He spoke as if I had reached the finish line.

Daughter, you did it, he said. *You got your associate's degree. I know you're happy to be done.*

I smiled, still wearing my cap and gown, and replied, *Oh no, Dad. I'm not done. I'm going back for my bachelor's degree.*

He looked at me in disbelief, probably wondering how I had the strength to do more when I had already done so much. But even then, I knew this wasn't the end. It was just another beginning.

"Strength does not come from winning. Your struggles develop your strengths. When you go through hardships and de-

cide not to surrender, that is strength." - Arnold Schwarzenegger

At this point, you, my readers, have journeyed with me more than halfway through this memoir. And here, I wanted this chapter to lighten the mood just a bit. The chapters before it are heavy, filled with trauma and pain, because that was my truth as I lived it and wrote it. But I wanted to pause here, right in the middle of the journey, to remind you that growth can happen even in survival mode.

I was building a career, raising children, fighting to survive, and learning who I was meant to be, all at the same time. And if I could do it, I want you to know that you can too. Do not allow your current or past circumstances to dictate what comes next. Your *next* is closer than you think. That next degree. That next career opportunity. That next season, filled with hope and possibility.

Even in my pain, I found reasons to stand. And I thank God that I don't look like what I've been through. When you see me now, I hope you see strength. I hope you see peace, joy, and perseverance. And most of all, I hope you see the light, the love of Jesus Christ, shining through everything I touch.

A Prayer for the one who feels Stuck

Father God,
I lift up every person who has just read this last chapter and may feel stuck. Stuck in circumstance, stuck in doubt, or just stuck in a season that feels heavier than they imagined it would be.

God, You see them. You see the weight they carry in silence. You see the responsibilities no one else acknowledges. You see the dreams they've placed on hold because survival demanded their attention. I ask You now to meet them exactly where they are.

Give strength to the weary. Give courage to the fearful. And give clarity to the confused. Restore hope to the places that disappointment tried to claim.

For the one questioning if it's too late, remind them that You are a God of restoration. For the one afraid to start again, remind them that You specialize in new beginnings. For the one battling doubt, silence every lie that tells them they are not enough.

Lord, reorder their steps. Give them wisdom to move forward and peace to rest when they need to pause. Let them know that their past does not disqualify them, their setbacks do not define them, and their current season does not determine their outcome. Replace doubt with trust in You. And when needed, be their strength.

In Jesus' name,
Amen

Chapter

13

My Full Circle Moment

Earlier on, in one of the previous chapters, I reflected on my own "daddy issues" and the hopes and dreams I had for my older three children, my first batch. Over the years, I tried to guide them carefully: monitoring who they spent time with, how they spent their evenings, and who came into our home.

On the surface, it might have looked like good parenting, but I know now that much of it came from a deeper place, my own unresolved trauma. I feared they would end up in situations I had experienced: young mothers with children from different fathers, or a young boy trying to raise a child still underdeveloped. I feared they would end up living lives I wished I had avoided. I never intended this for myself, yet I did what I could with what I knew at the time.

You've probably heard the saying: "Tell God your plans, and He will laugh." I thought I had it all figured out. My plan was simple, easy, and nearly complete: my first three children would grow, thrive, and avoid the mistakes I had made. At some point, the oldest two were in their early twenties, my youngest daughter was a teenager, and all I could think was, *Two down, one to go.* I held my breath, hoping she would reach adulthood without the label of "teen mother." I just knew she would move away to college soon and do all the things I wish I could have.

Then.... At the speed of light, something happened! One rainy Saturday, she came to me and asked if we could go to IHOP for breakfast. At first, I didn't think anything of it; I'd always made time to spend separately with each of my children. But once we got to the restaurant, she didn't waste a second. As soon as we ordered and the waitress walked away, she leaned in and said quietly, *I'm pregnant,* while holding up her phone with the picture of the test.

My heart dropped.

No... you're only sixteen. Still in high school.

An overwhelming mix of shock, fear, and sorrow washed over me. My first thought was, *How could you do this to me?* I made it about myself in that moment, drowning in the memories of my own pain.

No one knew the vow I had made to myself years before. I was so serious when I vowed that none of my children would ever face the struggles of teen parenting that I had endured. And here I am, slapped with this news. Devastation is an understatement.

To everyone else, I must have looked like just another angry parent. But the truth was so much more complicated than that. I felt like a failure. How could I have let this happen right under my nose?

Transitioning into the role of "Mom Mom" was an emotional roller coaster, to say the least. My daughter's pregnancy stirred up wounds I thought I had buried, forcing me to question myself: *Am I projecting my own pain onto her? Why does this hurt so deeply?* The triggers came in waves, days, weeks, even years of unresolved trauma rising to the surface all at once.

During that season, I found myself doubling up on therapy sessions just to stay afloat. Those appointments became the places where I could finally breathe again, the moments where I wasn't suffocating under the weight of fear, shame, and disappointment.

Therapy helped realign me. It gave me new tools, tools I desperately needed for this unexpected season ahead. The shift shook my confidence in ways that are still difficult to fully put into words.

I didn't want this for my children, especially my daughters. And with her being the baby of my first batch, the feeling of failure cut even deeper. Yet, even in that storm of emotion, God held my hand and guided me through it.

The early days of my daughter's pregnancy were rocky, but over time, His peace began to settle in, reminding me gently that His plans are higher, wiser, and more intentional than the ones I tried so hard to create on my own.

"For I know the plans I have for you," declares the Lord, "plans to prosper you and not to harm you, plans to give you hope and a future." - Jeremiah 29:11

This verse became my anchor. Originally spoken to God's people in exile, when their lives had not turned out as they hoped, it reminded me that even in seasons of devastation and uncertainty, God's hand is still at work. He is shaping us, guiding us, and preparing us for what is ahead. And as the season continued, my prayer became, "Lord, let Your will be done, not my own."

My full circle moment came in early 2025, when both my two daughters and grandson moved out into the home my older children had grown up in. It was my first home of my own, the same home I spoke about in chapter eight, the same home where

I had discovered I was pregnant with my third child, my second daughter. One afternoon, sitting in the car with my husband, I realized the full significance: my daughter was now twenty, the same age I had been when I first moved into that home.

"God's timing is perfect. His plans are higher than ours, and His love never fails." - Lysa TerKeurst

That full circle moment hit me with clarity. God had been at work, weaving our lives together in ways I could never have imagined. That little house, which I had held onto for twenty years, was now a stepping stone for my daughters and grandson, a place of hope, love, and new beginnings. Even through the guilt and shame of the seasons before, this was a new chapter of transformation and grace.

Looking back, I realize I may have been strict about education, boundaries, waiting to have sex, and making certain choices. I pray that my children now understand why I felt so strongly. Seeing my grandson take his first breath brought an unfamiliar kind of love, one I could not have predicted. It was a mix of heartbreak and joy, a painful yet beautiful reminder of life's cyclical nature. In the quiet still moments, I surrendered all my cares to the Lord.

"Cast all your anxiety on Him because He cares for you." – 1 Peter 5:7

Even as I wrestled with disappointment and fear, I felt God's reassurance that my children, my family, and I are all held in His care. His grace covers the mistakes, the fears, and the pain, allowing us to grow and heal, and watching my daughters now as adult women fills me with gratitude.

Our bonds and relationships have deepened since they moved out, and as Mom Mom, I get to support my youngest daughter through her journey in parenthood. God's guidance has allowed me to be a presence in her life in a way I never had at her age, and it has brought a sense of closure and fulfillment to my own journey.

"Come to me, all you who are weary and burdened, and I will give you rest." - Matthew 11:28

This journey with my children, the pain, the lessons, the victories, and the moments of grace, revealed to me that generational patterns don't have to define us. They exist to be acknowledged, faced, and transformed. What once seemed inevitable can be interrupted through awareness, love, and faith.

When asked how I survived this experience, honestly, the answer is layered. It was the grace that carried me through, which was not found in one place alone. It was the steady work of therapy paired with the sustaining healing power of Jesus. Even in the moments that felt devastating, God was working.

What I once saw as failure became an opportunity for redemption, for growth, and for the healing of generational patterns. My younger daughter now has me to guide her, to share wisdom and support, and to ensure that she experiences what I didn't always have at her age: loving guidance, patience, and grace.

As I reflect on this journey, I see clearly how unhealed pain can follow us into relationships, parenting, and daily life. Yet, I also see that God's intervention allows cycles to break, hearts to heal, and wisdom to be passed forward. This awareness leads naturally to the next step in my story, examining the generational trauma responses that have shaped our family, the patterns that we can now recognize, and the ways we can intentionally change for future generations.

A Prayer for Grace over our Children

Dear Heavenly Father,
Thank You for Your faithfulness, even when life doesn't go as planned. Thank You for guiding me through the pain, the mistakes, and the seasons of fear that have come with raising my children.

Lord God, I lift up my daughters to You now, especially my youngest as she navigates the path of motherhood. May Your wisdom, protection, and grace cover her every step.

Lord, I pray for my heart, for patience, for understanding, and for forgiveness. Help me release the guilt of the past and the mistakes I thought I made, and to embrace Your plan for our family.

May my experiences serve as a testimony of Your love and guidance, not only for my children but for those who are reading this right now. Father, I ask for Your covering over every generational cycle of trauma.

Replace fear with faith, replace shame with grace, and replace pain with healing. Let all children who are a product of teen parenting walk boldly in the purpose You have prepared for them.

May the lessons I have learned be tools of encouragement rather than chains of regret.

Lord, I thank You for the full circle moments! The times that remind me how Your plans are always higher than mine, and Your timing is perfect. Continue to use our home, our lives, and our experiences as stepping stones for others who are seeking growth, transformation, and Liberty. May Your peace fill their hearts beyond understanding.

In Jesus' name,
Amen.

Chapter

14

Motherhood Lessons

I can look back now and say, *Being a young mother saved me from myself.* Those words hold the deepest truth of my life. When I was at my lowest, overwhelmed by shame, fear, and uncertainty, motherhood became my anchor, my reason to keep moving forward. Even in moments when giving up seemed easier, when the weight of my circumstances pressed down hard, something inside me refused to quit. That something was resilience. A quiet strength born out of necessity, love, and hope.

Teen motherhood taught me lessons I never expected. Patience, learning to slow down when everything inside me felt rushed and chaotic. Selflessness, putting someone else's needs above my own, even when I had very little to give. And unconditional love, the kind that doesn't fade in hard times but grows stronger with every sleepless night, every sacrifice, and every moment, I wasn't sure I was doing it right.

Life, however, didn't slow down. In fact, it moved at the speed of light. Every day demanded something different from me, wisdom I didn't yet have, strength I had to borrow, and courage I prayed for constantly. Teenage motherhood forced me to grow up fast, to make decisions I wasn't prepared for, and to face realities that many of my age never had to think about. But even in the chaos, I was learning. I was being shaped. I was discovering who I was and who God was calling me to become.

As you have read, my earlier years were incredibly difficult, mentally, emotionally, spiritually, and financially. I was young, overwhelmed, and stretched thin, but I was also determined. Looking back, I can honestly say those experiences didn't destroy me; they deepened me. They shaped my faith in a way that was real, raw, and lasting. I learned to lean fully on the strength of God. Scriptures like Philippians 4:13 became more than just words; I lived them:

"I can do all things through Christ who strengthens me."
- Philippians 4:13

Through each season of uncertainty, I was reminded of my identity, not just as a young mother doing her best, but as a believer. A child of God. My experiences, as heavy as they were, laid the foundation of my faith walk. And that faith carried me through storms I never imagined I could survive.

That's the heart of this book's title. My journey wasn't just about becoming a teenage mom; it was about becoming a woman. A woman who learned, stumbled, broke down at times, but always stood back up. A woman who discovered strength she didn't know she had, resilience she didn't remember learning, and wisdom she didn't know she carried. And through it all, my faith was my lifeline. When I couldn't find the words to pray, God was still there, holding me steady. His word reminded me that even when I am weak, He intercedes for me:

"In the same way, the Spirit helps us in our weakness. We do not know what we ought to pray for, but the Spirit himself intercedes for us through wordless groans. And he who searches our hearts knows the mind of the Spirit, because the Spirit intercedes for God's people in accordance with the will of God."- Romans 8:26–27

I leaned on His promises during my darkest days, and they gave me peace and purpose. Jeremiah 29:11 reminded me that even when my circumstances felt impossible, God had a plan bigger than my pain:

"For I know the plans I have for you," declares the Lord, plans to prosper you and not to harm you, plans to give you hope and a future." -Jeremiah 29:11

And even when I couldn't see how things would work out, Romans 8:28 reassured me that God was working behind the scenes:

"And we know that in all things God works for the good of those who love Him, who have been called according to His purpose."- Romans 8:28

On the days I felt empty, broken, or exhausted, this verse carried me:

"My flesh and my heart may fail, but God is the strength of my heart and my portion forever." - Psalm 73:26

By now, motherhood held up a mirror, and for the first time, I had to face what was reflecting back. And that's when I began to understand something I had never been taught: you can't parent from healed places if you've never allowed yourself to heal.

Before I could break cycles for my children, I had to recognize the ones that lived in me.

As you have discovered at the beginning of this memoir, my story didn't begin with me becoming a teen mother; it began long before that. Deep inside, I was a young girl searching for stability, love, and a sense of belonging. And whether I realized it or not, those unspoken wounds followed me into each season of my life.

Through raising my children, I was raising myself at the same time. In many ways, it was the blind leading the blind, and yet, we all pretty much grew up together.

And when I say *we*, I mean more than just my children. My mother and I grew up together. My stepfather and I grew up together. My father and I grew up together. But most importantly, my children, my first batch, my rhythm of heartbeats, the ones I got to learn with, the ones I learned *through*, we truly did grow up together.

A Prayer for the Teen Mother Finding Her Way

Dear God,
I never imagined motherhood would find me this soon.
Some days I still feel like a child myself, unsure, afraid, and reaching for pieces of a world that used to feel simple.

Lord, although I am grieving what I lost, let me not forget the blessings you have provided. My childhood is no longer, my freedom looks different, but I have the ease of just knowing that you are right by my side.

In the quiet hours, when the house is still and my baby breathes against my chest, I sense You there with me, Oh Lord! Whispering to me, letting me know that this is not the end of my story, It's the beginning of a new chapter.

In spite of what it looks like, I am thankful you see me. You see me as chosen. You see me as capable. You see me as loved. Lord, help me walk into tomorrow without shame, but with boldness.

Help me to see myself through your lens. And remind me that Your favor still covers me even when I feel out of place, even when I'm learning to be both a girl and a mother.

Let Your grace fill the gaps where my strength runs out. Teach me to see the beauty in it all and to trust that You are shaping me through every sleepless night, every tear, every tender moment.

In the mighty name of Jesus, I pray
Amen.

Chapter

15

Generational Trauma Responses

Is it possible to break a cycle you were born into? That question stayed with me long before I even had the words to ask it out loud. Somewhere deep inside, I always sensed I was carrying more than just my own story. It felt like I was living out patterns that had been set long before I took my first breath. For a while, I didn't question it, I just lived it. But the more I grew, especially after becoming a mother, the more I realized that what we don't heal, we often hand down.

In many ways, I was born into a story already in progress. In my family, teen pregnancy wasn't shocking; it was familiar. My mother had me at sixteen, and there's no doubt in my mind that this wasn't a new chapter for our bloodline. It was more like a rerun. And then there was substance use.

Growing up, I saw the effects of alcohol and drugs firsthand. I witnessed how they were used to numb pain, escape reality, or get through the day. There wasn't much conversation about it, just quiet acceptance, like it was something to live with, not something to question.

Another cycle? Emotional silence. We didn't talk about what hurt us. We didn't unpack our pain. We moved through life like nothing happened, even when everything did. That silence became normal, and over time, I internalized it. I believed that staying quiet made me strong, that asking for help meant I was weak. I learned to keep things in, to stay small, and to pretend I was okay even when I wasn't.

When I became a mother, those cycles didn't just disappear. In fact, they showed up louder. And that's when I started to recognize something even deeper: I had trauma responses I didn't even know were trauma. I found myself overthinking everything- conversations, decisions, even the smallest interactions. I was always trying to prepare for the worst. And don't get on my bad side, or you would hear my mouth in the fighting kind of way.

I bent over backward to keep people happy, often at the cost of my own peace. I avoided conflict because I didn't want to be misunderstood or rejected. I was reacting to things in the present, but those reactions were rooted in pain from the past. It was through reflection and a lot of spiritual growth that I came to realize these patterns weren't my fault, but they were my responsibility. I couldn't change where I came from, but I could decide where I was going. I could be the one who said, *This stops with me.*

We often hear the phrase *"generational curse",* the idea that certain struggles, patterns, or pain can pass down from one generation to the next. As I reflect on my own childhood and teenage years, I can't ignore the repeated pattern of teen pregnancy in my family. Becoming a teen mother didn't fall far from the tree. And if I looked even further into my family history, I'm almost certain I'd find others who had children just as young, if not younger, than I did.

My mother became pregnant with me at just sixteen. Neither she nor my father had the tools, knowledge, or emotional readiness to raise a child. And yet, here I am. I wasn't born into a picture-perfect family, or into a home fully prepared for parenthood, but I know now, more than ever, that I was not a mistake. God was intentional when He created me. He saw me long before I was formed and had already woven purpose into my life.

"I praise you because I am fearfully and wonderfully made; your works are wonderful, I know that full well." - Psalm

139:14

Science backs this up. There's real research around something called generational trauma, the idea that pain and survival behaviors can be passed down through families if they go unaddressed. I didn't know that when I was in it. All I knew was that I didn't want to repeat history; I wanted to rewrite it. Not just for my children, but for myself. I wanted to choose love over shame. Honesty over silence. Growth over survival.

Even now, I catch myself falling into old habits. I still have moments of overthinking. I still catch myself biting my tongue when I want to speak up. But now, I notice it. And that awareness, that pause, is where healing starts. I'm not perfect, but I'm present. And that makes all the difference.

We don't heal by pretending our past didn't happen. We heal by naming it, owning it, and deciding it no longer gets to own us. For me, true healing began the moment I stopped trying to carry everything alone.

Jesus and therapy became the lifeline I didn't know I needed, one for my soul, the other for my mind. God gave me the wisdom to seek help, the courage to face what I had buried, and the strength to keep showing up even when it hurt.

My consistency, my willingness to fight for my freedom, and

my choice to stay committed to healing have been some of the best decisions I've ever made. God guided me step by step, meeting me in prayer, in sessions, in quiet moments, and in hard truths.

The cycle can end here. The silence can stop with us. Because we are not cursed, we are chosen, equipped, and empowered to be the change.

"Do not conform to the pattern of this world, but be transformed by the renewing of your mind. Then you would be able to test and approve what Gods will is, his good, pleasing and perfect will." - Romans 12:2

The truth is, healing isn't just about who you're trying not to become; it's also about who and what you're fighting for. Maybe, as you read this, you already know what that reason is, or maybe you're still discovering it. Either way, the search itself matters. For me, that reason was my children. They became my motivation, my anchor, and the constant reminder that even though life didn't go as planned, I still had purpose.

A Prayer for Breaking Generational Cycles

Father God,

Thank You for opening my eyes to see the patterns I once called "normal." For so long, I carried pain that wasn't mine to keep. I inherited silence and fear. My survival mode was on repeat. But Lord, You are teaching me to trade in my tears for truth, courage, and peace.

I no longer want to live from my wounds. I want to live from the healing You promised. You showed me that what was passed down through generations can be transformed through revelation.

You are breaking chains I didn't even know existed. I thank You for trusting me to be the one who says, "It stops here." I release the stories that tried to define me. I forgive what I once resented.

May my life be proof that curses can turn into callings, and that with You, God, no history is too heavy to be healed. I bless the generations before me for doing the best they could, and I pray healing over the generations that will come after me.

In Jesus' name I pray,
Amen

Chapter

16

Memory Lane

So... you might be wondering: Why did I take this stroll?

Honestly, I realized, no matter how scary it initially felt, it was the only way to unpack. I realized the story of my past still had a pulse of its own. I realized my story was never mine to keep. I realized that God didn't bring me through it just to bury it. And, eventually, I realized it was my only way forward.

Memory Lane is often described as a sweet, quiet place, a soft walk-through childhood laughter, familiar smells, old songs, and the little moments that shaped who we became.
From my experience, people would talk about it like it's always peaceful, like it always leads to warmth and nostalgia.
For me, though, going down Memory Lane wasn't about chasing sentimental moments. It was important because I needed to

understand the pieces of myself I had tucked away. I had spent so many years surviving that I never slowed down long enough to truly see what had shaped me, what hurt me, what grew me, and what still needed healing.

Writing this book forced me to stop avoiding those places. I knew that if I wanted real restoration, real forgiveness, and real freedom, I had to go back and face the parts of my story I once walked past with my eyes closed. This journey wasn't a trip I wanted to take, but it became one I needed in my desperate attempt to move forward in this journey of wholeness.

When I say Memory Lane, I don't mean a scrapbook of perfectly framed pictures. I mean the real thing, the good, the bad, the blurry, the beautiful, and the broken. I mean, the places where I grew up too fast. The rooms where I cried quietly. The houses we stayed in, only long enough to pack again. The moments where my parents, teenagers themselves, were fighting their own battles with addiction while trying to raise children in the middle of their storms. I mean the nights where I prayed for stability while we moved from relative to relative, carrying the kind of fear a child shouldn't know. I mean the moment I became a mother at fourteen, still a child myself, holding a baby and a burden I never had time to prepare for.

Yes, Memory Lane holds all of that, but it also holds something else: the pieces of me I thought I lost. And that's why I had to walk through it.

I've heard people say that strolling down memory lane will only be a reminder of who we used to be, but for me, it became a reminder of who God protected me to become. It reminded me of the girl I was before life hardened her, before responsibility settled on her shoulders like a weight too heavy to name. It reminded me of the moments that shaped my softness, my worry, my observing nature, and the quiet way I learned to carry pain. It reminded me that even when I didn't know God, God knew me. Even when I didn't understand my story, He was writing it with a steady hand while touching wounds only He can reach.

"He heals the brokenhearted and binds up their wounds." - Psalm 147:3

Overall, walking down the footsteps of my past while writing this Broken Glass series was not a smooth stroll. Thus far, it has been slow and tender, and at times it felt like picking up shattered pieces without wanting to cut myself again.

Silent stillness seems easier, safer, but then again, I realized you can't heal from what you refuse to look at. You can't forgive what you won't name. You can't grow from what you pretend never happened.

I had to sit with the girl I used to be, the one who cried in the schoolyard when that bee stung her ear, the one who didn't know that life would sting even harder later. I had to sit with the little girl who was violated without warning. I had to sit with the teenager who tried her best to hide her tears while figuring out motherhood. I had to sit with the teenager, looking for love in all the wrong places and sexual validation due to her daddy issues. I had to sit with the young woman who felt bruised by life but somehow kept getting up every morning. And as I walked through those memories, God sat with me. Every step. Every flashback. Every ache.

This walk down Memory Lane stopped being just a place of pain and became a place of release. With God seated with me on the journey, I didn't just revisit the past; I started forgiving it. I started to forgive the people in it. And for the sake of true restoration, eventually, I started to forgive myself.

"Come to me, all you who are weary and burdened, and I will give you rest." - Matthew 11:28

Some people think healing means forgetting, but I've learned healing means remembering differently, not with shame, not with anger, but with understanding, compassion, and grace. Grace for my current self, grace for the ones who hurt me, and grace for the little girl who survived what should have broken her.

Restoration has become my portion in this season. God continues to meet me in places I once avoided, showing me that what tried to break me ended up building me, and that broken glass still reflects light in its own way.

As this chapter closes, I want to take time to thank the Lord because I know it's because of Him that this journey ahead is possible.

Thank You, Father, for being the God who heals, the God who restores, the God who turns brokenness into beauty. Thank You for transforming my walk down Memory Lane into a path toward freedom. Lord, let every reader feel hope rising, grace covering, and Your love leading them forward, one step, one memory, one moment at a time.

A Prayer for the Road Behind and the Healing Ahead

Father God,

I come before You with a heart full of gratitude.

Thank You for carrying me through every season of my life; through the chaos, the instability, the nights filled with fear, and the mornings where strength showed up even when I didn't know how it arrived.

Thank You for walking with me through every hidden memory, every unspoken ache, every chapter I once tried to bury deep inside myself.

Lord, You have been faithful. You have been steady. You have been present even when I mistook Your silence for absence. And today, as I looked back down Memory Lane, I thank You for giving me the courage to revisit what once felt too heavy to face.

God, You know every step of the journey that shaped me. You saw the little girl who prayed for peace, the teenager who felt life pressing in too quickly, and the young mother who held a baby at an age when she still needed to be held herself.

Through all of it, Lord, You kept me. You protected me. You preserved the parts of me I once believed were lost. Thank You for giving me the strength to return to those memories, not to relive the pain, but to release it.

Thank You for allowing me to see my story through Your eyes, with compassion instead of shame and with grace instead of guilt. Thank You for reminding me that healing does not require forgetting, but remembering differently, with a softer heart and a renewed understanding of the girl I used to be.

Thank You for meeting me in the places I avoided, and for showing me that every broken piece, every silent wound, every tear I tried to hide was held in Your hands the entire time.

In Jesus Name,
Amen

Chapter

17

Purpose, Faith, and your Journey Forward

Life didn't stop because I became a mom. It started over. I often say that my children saved my life, not because everything got easier, but because for the first time, I had something greater than myself to live for.

As a first-time teen mother, my son learned how to walk, while I learned how to stand up for myself. He said his first words while I found my voice again. At first glance, he gave me a reason to heal, to fight, and to believe that God hadn't forgotten about me.

I think back sometimes to the little girl I was, the one standing in line at school, proud of her gold stud earrings, not knowing a bee was about to sting her. She cried so hard that day. Not just because it hurt, but because it was the first time she realized that pain could come out of nowhere. I wish I could go back and tell her that won't be the last time something stings. But you'll survive them all. Little Thelma, you'll carry the hurt, yes, but you'll also carry the strength it gave you. That sting didn't break you. None of them did.

"You only understand people if you feel them in yourself"
– John Steinbeck

Shifting it back to you, my reader, even if you were not or have never been a teenage mother, and you're holding this book and wondering if you'll ever get through your own storm, let me remind you: *you already are.*

Now, after walking down Memory Lane with me, I want you to understand something: your past doesn't have to define your future. Seeing my own story in all its brokenness and beauty reminded me that healing is possible. I realized that no matter how chaotic, how unfair, or how painful life may have been, God has been walking with me through it all. Every mistake, every loss, every sleepless night, He was there, shaping me, strengthening me, and preparing me for what is to come. And He has that same patience, that same faithfulness, for you.

When you look back at your own life, don't be afraid of what you might see. Don't shy away from the moments that sting or the memories that make you flinch. They are not there to punish you; they are there to teach you, to guide you, and to remind you how far you've come. However, if you're not quite ready for such a step, know that's ok too. I want you to pause here and recognize the courage it takes to keep going. The courage it takes to rise, to choose purpose over fear, to choose faith over despair. That courage is yours, and it has been there all along, quietly waiting for you to claim it.

Know that every day you wake up and keep going, you're choosing to break generational cycles. You're choosing to fight back by overcoming your fears. You're choosing purpose over sobbing in your pain. Remember, you don't have to be perfect to be powerful. And you don't have to have it all together to be a good human being. I hope you see the resilience in yourself somewhere in these pages. I hope you know just how much you are loved. You are special, and you matter. I hope you feel less alone. And I pray that by the time you reach this page, you realize just how far you've come, and how much further you can go.

So, to every person who took the time to read my memoir, whether you are, or were, a young mother, a young father, or even if you are not a parent, know this: You are not alone. The path you walk may be tough and uncertain, but you can rise.

You can dream big. You can build a life filled with love, purpose, and joy. Because you have breath in your lungs, your story isn't over; in fact, it's just beginning. Hold tight to your faith, lean on those who love you, and remember: every step forward is a victory.

As I offer these final words, I want to leave you with this reminder: healing takes time, and it only unfolds when you are ready. Give yourself grace. Be patient with your process. If you are not ready to unpack everything, that is okay, too. There is no rush. Choose quiet moments to sit with God, to lay it before Him, even if all you can offer is silence. In the right timing, healing will take place.

Remember that your journey forward is sacred. It is yours to shape, to nurture, and to honor. God is still writing your story, and every step you take toward healing, forgiveness, and purpose is part of the masterpiece only He can create. If you decide to dig at all, do so gently, offering yourself grace and moving at your own pace.

Because even broken glass, when held to the light, still shines. And even a sting, once so sharp, becomes proof that you're still standing.

A Prayer for Every Wounded Heart Turning These Pages

Father God,
I lift up every reader who is holding this book. Every soul who has walked through storms they never asked for, who carries memories they still don't have words for, who has tucked away pieces of themselves to survive.

Father, You know their pasts, their pain, their hidden fears, and their silent prayers. I pray that as they journey through these pages, something inside them begins to soften.

Should you see fit, I pray that You give them courage to face what they've pushed aside. Give them clarity where there has been confusion. Please give them a holy, steady strength, the kind that doesn't rush healing but invites it gently.

For the reader who has wounds they've never named, Lord, make room for honesty.
For the one whose memories feel like too much to carry, bring a peace that steadies their breath.
For the one who has been running from their past or running from themselves, slow them down long enough to feel seen.

And Lord, when the time is right, Your time, not others, not theirs, but Yours, please give them the strength to unpack what they have held so tightly.

Show them that healing is not a punishment, but a promise. A promise that restoration is possible. A promise that they do not have to walk their Memory Lane alone. A promise that their story still has purpose.

God, as they heal, I ask that You bless their future. Let their future be lighter than their past. Let it be covered in Your peace, guided by Your wisdom, and shaped by the kind of hope that rises even after long nights of heaviness.
Father God, lead them into days where joy feels reachable again, where rest comes easier, and where they begin to trust themselves, and You more deeply than ever before.

In Jesus' name,
Amen

A Message: Parenthood Before They Were Ready!

Dear You,

I see you. I see your fears, your doubts, your struggles, and your incredible strength. Being a teen parent is hard, but it's also an opportunity to rewrite your story. You are capable of more than you realize.

Your dreams matter. Your child needs you, and you need to take care of yourself, too.
Keep going.
Keep growing.
You are never alone in this journey.
Read these affirmations out loud:

- *I am doing the best I can- and that is more than enough.*
- *I am growing every day- and so is my strength.*
- *My past does not define me!*
- *I am creating a new future.*
- *God is with me in every moment, even the hard ones.*
- *I am capable*
- *I am chosen*
- *I am loved*
- *Even when I feel alone, I am never abandoned*
- *I am rewriting my story, one day at a time.*

With love and hope,
Thelma

"There is no greater agony than bearing an untold story inside you."
--Maya Angelou

Author's Note:

A visual: Becoming Thelma

Can you believe we have made it to the end of this first segment of my life? I'm still in disbelief myself!

As my readers, you are my family now.
And for that, I wanted to give a token of my love and appreciation for journeying with me through these first few layers of healing. As you turn the next page, I invite you into a visual memory of my past. These photos are more than images; they are pieces of the journey I've shared with you in these pages. You'll see the little girl I once was, the teenager growing up far too soon, and the young mother learning, step by step, how to stand in her own strength.

I wanted to share a deeper look into who I was and who I have become. These pictures are tender and dear to me. Some represent "Nay Nay" some represent "Renee," and some represent my growth to becoming "Thelma". Some make me smile, some bring tears, and others invite quiet reflection. But, all and all, I have learned to embrace each one. They honor the path I walked and the resilience God built in me along the way. They hold pieces of my becoming, pieces I once hid, but now reveal with transparency, courage, and grace.

As you look through them, I hope you feel a sense of connection, not only to my story, but to the parts of your own story of becoming. The parts in you that have survived, grown, and are still carrying the strength needed for your own next.

Standing here at the end of this first book in the *Broken Glass* series, I feel a peace I did not expect. Not because my past has changed, because Lord knows I still have plenty of work to do, but because I finally stopped letting it define how I see myself. I walked back through what was. I survived it. I learned from it. And I am still healing through it.

Thank you for taking this first step toward freedom with me.

With humility, gratitude, and love,
Thelma

"To be rooted is perhaps the most important and least recognized need of the human soul." -- Simone Weil

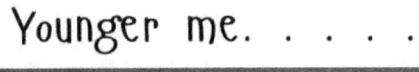 Younger me. . . . .

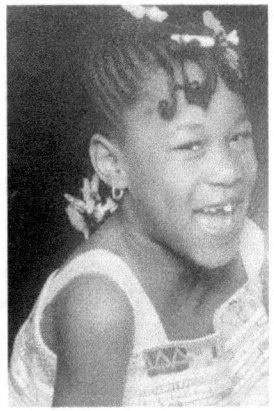

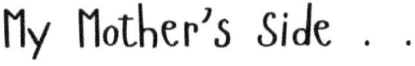

My Father's Side . . . .

Me & My Heartbeats. . . .

To My Readers

A Special Thank You to My Readers

From the bottom of my heart, I wanted to take this time to personally thank you all for taking this walk with me and reading book one, *We Grew Up Together*. Writing this particular memoir was both a journey of healing and reflection. It was a way to give a voice to the young girl I once was and to honor the woman I have become. If you've walked with me through these pages, you've shared in the laughter, the tears, the doubt, and the triumphs. Your willingness to listen means more than words can express. My heart is so full.

For every teenage parent, every young woman searching for her strength, every young boy searching for his identity, and every person who has ever had to grow up faster than expected, this story was for you! May you be reminded that no matter where your journey began, God's grace can meet you there. Deep down within, you have the strength to overcome.

"She is clothed with strength and dignity, and she laughs without fear of the future." - Proverbs 31:25

With love and gratitude,
Thelma

Acknowledgments

To start, I acknowledge my Lord and Savior, Jesus Christ, who is first in my life. In addition, I know in my heart the completion of this memoir would not have been possible without the love, support, and encouragement of many people who stood beside me over the last eight years as I poured my truth onto these pages.

To my husband, Coley L. Clanton, thank you again for being my daily strength and safe space. Your patience and love carried me through long nights of doubt and pushed me to finish strong. To my children and grandson, your lives are my inspiration. Thank you for allowing me to grow with you and for giving me purpose every day. To my parents, grandparents, and in-laws, your prayers, life lessons, and presence have anchored me more than you know. I honor you in these pages.

To my friends, my mentors, my Pastoral Leadership, and spiritual family who have spoken life over me, thank you for reminding me that my story matters. Your words helped me press forward. To every teen parent, every young woman and man who has felt broken, unseen, or unworthy, this book is for you. Thank you for inspiring me to keep writing, keep healing, and keep believing.
May this book be a reminder that no matter how your story starts, it's never too late to write a new ending.

In Loving Memory

A Letter to my Grandparents

To my grandparents who are resting peacefully,
I love you.
Even those whom I didn't get to meet personally, in many ways, I have witnessed your love, wisdom, and unwavering support through my parents.

Thank you for being an important part of shaping the person I am today. Though you are no longer with us, your spirit lives deep within my heart and in every step I take forward toward liberty and healing.

Forever in my heart, always in my thoughts,
Thelma

In Loving Memory

Grandmothers	Sunrise	Sunset
Eloise Gretrue (True) Allen	12/15/1932	unknown/1993
Eloise (NaNa) Allen	5/9/1915	8/1/2010
Dorothy May "Greyhouse" McKnight	6/16/1918or20	8/23/2014
Thelma Allen	9/18/1949	12/28/2022
Bessie Holiday "Nana" Canty	4/4/unknown	1/27/2011
Julia Ann Davis	1/18/1946	7/4/1987
Moncia (Monnie) Evangeline Foster-Holloman	4/4/1914	3/17/2012
Mary Lee Duckrey	7/31/1933	2/9/2025
Daisy Mae Simmons	6/19/1914	6/10/1989
Vivian Washington	11/28/1938	12/8/2017
Grandfathers	**Sunrise**	**Sunset**
Morris Allen	6/23/1948	1/29/2000
Charles James McCrae	2/11/1925	9/1/1968
Coley D. Clanton	5/25/1938	5/21/1988

Scripture Index

Deuteronomy 31:8 (NIV) -- *The Lord himself goes before you and will be with you; he will never leave you nor forsake you. (Ch.).*

Joshua 1:9 (NIV) -- *Be strong and courageous. Do not be afraid; do not be discouraged, for the Lord your God will be with you wherever you go. (Ch.).*

Psalm 23:4 (NIV) -- *Even when I walk through the darkest valley, I will not be afraid, for you are close beside me. Your rod and your staff protect and comfort me. (Ch. 3).*

Psalm 34:5 (NIV) -- *Those who look to him are radiant; their faces are never covered with shame. (Ch.).*

Psalm 34:18 (NIV) -- *The Lord is close to the brokenhearted and saves those who are crushed in spirit. (Reflection).*

Psalm 40:2–3 (NIV) -- *He lifted me out of the slimy pit, out of the mud and mire; he set my feet on a rock and gave me a firm place to stand. He put a new song in my mouth, a hymn of praise to our God. (Cp. 3).*

Psalm 51:17 (NIV) -- *My sacrifice, O God, is a broken spirit; a broken and contrite heart you, God, will not despise. (Series intro)*

Psalm 73:26 (NIV) -- *My flesh and my heart may fail, but God is the strength of my heart and my portion forever. (Ch.).*

Psalm 86:15 (NIV) – *But you, Lord, are a compassionate and gracious God, slow to anger, abounding in love and faithfulness. (Ch. 4).*

Psalm 139:1 (NIV) -- *You have searched me, Lord, and you know me. (Ch.).*

Psalm 139:14 (NIV) -- *I praise you because I am fearfully and wonderfully made; your works are wonderful, I know that full well. (Ch. 15).*

Psalm 147:3 (NIV) -- *He heals the brokenhearted and binds up their wounds. (Ch. 1 & 16).*

Proverbs 31:25 (NIV) -- *She is clothed with strength and dignity, and she laughs without fear of the future. (Thank you)*

Isaiah 43:2 (NIV) -- *When you pass through the waters, I will be with you. (Book Intro).*

Isaiah 61:1 (NIV) -- *The Spirit of the Sovereign Lord is on me, because the Lord has anointed me to proclaim good news to the poor. He has sent me to bind up the brokenhearted, to proclaim freedom for the captives and release from darkness for the prisoners. (Ch.).*

Isaiah 66:9 (NIV) -- *Do I bring to the moment of birth and not give delivery? says the Lord. Do I close up the womb when I bring to delivery? says your God. (Ch.).*

Jeremiah 29:11 (NIV) -- *For I know the plans I have for you," declares the Lord, "plans to prosper you and not to harm you, plans to give you hope and a future. (Ch. 13).*

Jeremiah 29:13 (NIV) -- *You will seek me and find me when you seek me with all your heart. (Ch.).*

Jeremiah 31:3 (NIV) -- *I have loved you with an everlasting love; I have drawn you with unfailing kindness. (Ch.).*

Ezekiel 36:26 (NIV) -- *I will give you a new heart and put a new spirit in you; I will remove from you your heart of stone and give you a heart of flesh. (Ch.).*

Matthew 11:28 (NIV) -- *Come to me, all you who are weary and burdened, and I will give you rest. (Ch. 16).*

John 8:32 (NIV) -- *Then you will know the truth, and the truth will set you free. (Ch. 2).*

Romans 8:26–27 (NIV) -- *In the same way, the Spirit helps us in our weakness. We do not know what we ought to pray for, but the Spirit himself intercedes for us through wordless groans. And he who searches our hearts knows the mind of the Spirit, because the Spirit intercedes for God's people in accordance with the will of God. (Ch.).*

Romans 8:28 (NIV) -- *And we know that in all things God works for the good of those who love him, who have been called according to his purpose. (Ch. 5).*

Romans 12:2 (NIV) -- *Do not conform to the pattern of this world, but be transformed by the renewing of your mind. Then you would be able to test and approve what Gods will is, his good, pleasing and perfect will. (Ch. 15).*

1 Corinthians 13:7 (NIV) -- *Love bears all things, believes all things, hopes all things, endures all things. (Ch. 5).*

2 Corinthians 4:8–9 (NIV) -- *We are hard pressed on every side, but not crushed; perplexed, but not in despair; persecuted, but not abandoned; struck down, but not destroyed. (Ch. 4).*

2 Corinthians 12:9 (NIV) -- *But he said to me, "My grace is sufficient for you, for my power is made perfect in weakness."*

Philippians 4:13 (NIV) -- *I can do all this through him who gives me strength. (Ch.).*

1 Peter 5:7 (NIV) -- *Cast all your anxiety on him because he cares for you. (Ch.).*

A Closing Prayer, just for YOU....

God,

I lift up every reader who sees themselves somewhere in this memoir. Every young mother or father, every overwhelmed parent, every person who stepped into responsibility before they felt prepared. I pray for the one who feels judged, unseen, or misunderstood. The ones who are learning to balance and juggle parent life, struggles, and trauma. The ones who are still walking through life feeling out of place, carrying burdens no one else knows about. Lord, breathe strength into them. Let them feel Your nearness in their exhaustion. Remind them that they are not failing, they are fighting, growing, and showing up with a brave kind of love that You honor deeply.

For the readers who are battling shame, remind them that shame has no authority where Your grace lives. For the readers carrying fear, anchor them in Your promise that You would never bring them to their next season or their purpose without carrying them through it. For the readers who feel torn between worlds, give them the wisdom to navigate their path. For the readers who struggle with the background noise, give them peace to silence the doubts and replace them with whispers from Your Holy Spirit.

And Father God, for the reader who feels alone, wrap them in your loving comfort. Surround them with the support they need to navigate their next. In Jesus' mighty name I pray, with Thanksgiving on my heart,
Amen

And, She's Still Becoming. . . . .

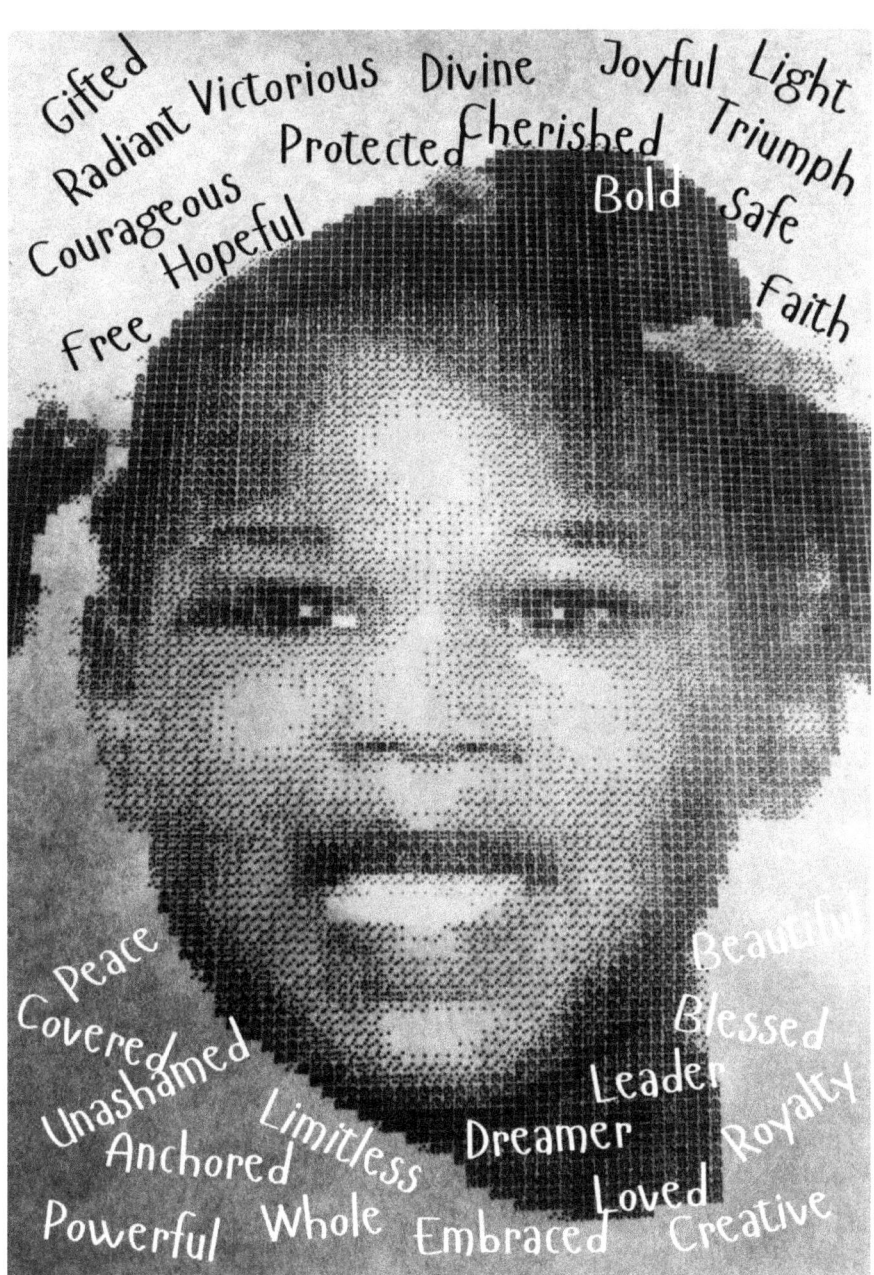

www.ingramcontent.com/pod-product-compliance
Lightning Source LLC
LaVergne TN
LVHW010217070526
838199LV00062B/4624